Funeral Home Marketing

Moving the Bottom Line

By Glenn H. Gould III
Chief Executive Officer, MKJ Marketing

FOREWORD

For over twenty years, MKJ Marketing has been assisting funeral home managers and owners to accomplish their marketing and advertising objectives. In recent years, I have come to notice how little the challenges have changed over this period. Some of the challenges may be more wide spread than they were early on, but they're fundamentally the same challenges.

During this period, MKJ Marketing has conducted over 700 research studies, and assisted over 2000 funeral homes throughout the United States, Canada, the United Kingdom, Australia, and South America. This book is a synopsis of the most important issues in funeral service.

©2010 by MKJ Marketing

All Rights Reserved. • Published by MKJ Marketing, Inc., Largo, FL

Table of contents

Contrary to popular opinion, the funeral profession has been dynamic in its efforts to keep pace with the changes in American culture.

Few industries would have fared as well as funeral service given the challenges the profession has faced over the past forty years. Although much of the credit for its survival can be attributed to the resilience of the family business, it must also be assumed that the American consumer perceives value in funeral services, even with the shift in society's priorities. Based upon the findings of hundreds of research studies and focus group sessions, Glenn Gould's second book, reveals the services and products today's consumers perceive of value. Marilyn Jones Gould has trained thousands of licensed funeral directors in at-need and pre-need communications skills. "Funeral Home Marketing" incorporates her experience working with funeral directors and funeral home owners in the implementation of these innovations.

Dedicated to my parents,
Glenn and Margaret Gould

CHAPTER 1

Death Care Marketing in the New Economy

For the first time since the mass marketing of credit began following WWII, American consumers are choosing not to accept credit, preferring instead to live on their available cash. According to an article authored by Mary Pilon on WSJ Blogs, *"As the credit-card industry reinvents itself amid a dismal economy and a new regulatory regimen, consumers are rebelling. They're going debit. Some 58.2% of card transactions are now paid for with debit cards, compared to 41.8% with credit cards, according to data from the Nilson Report. Debit cards now represent 38.3% of card dollars spent, compared to only 26% in 2002."*

It's difficult to conceptualize an American household actually living on the money they make. If there is any question that the recession of 2009 is having a profound impact on our society, the move from credit cards to debit dispels it. According to Ms. Pilon, ***"Part of debit's rise can be attributed to the overall tightening of credit. Part of it could also be consumers trying to use debit to manage their budgets more efficiently. One of the advantages of using a debit card is that it's virtually impossible to rack up debt."***

Although the growing popularity of debit cards is a significant indicator of American's change in attitudes, it is only one. Americans are taking control of their lives in many ways as they evaluate their positions and how they want to live. Americans are demanding smaller homes, fuel efficient automobiles, and lower interest rates on loans while shopping for better returns on their investments. They want to live longer, pay off their mortgages, and spend less. What does this mean for funeral service?

The declining birth rate during the depression years of the 1930's has resulted in a steady decline in the death rate beginning in the late 1990's. In the year 2000, 35 states had more deaths than the previous years while the number of deaths in 15 states declined. That means the out migration from 15 states increased the death rates in all the other states. The 15 "losing" states are clustered in the northeast and near midwest; in fact the only exceptions were Ohio and Wisconsin experiencing no change in the number of deaths.

Because of lost retirement savings due to the financial bust of 2008, the declining home values and the difficulty in selling homes to finance retirements in the Sunbelt states, people will be dying up north instead of Florida, Arizona and the Carolinas. Over the next decade the deaths will shift from retirement states back to the industrial northern states. Since many of the nation's funeral homes operate in the eastern industrial corridor, the most significant impact of the recession will be very visible and positive, but what other changes will the recession of 2009 bring to funeral service?

WSJ Blogs, The Wallet, Mary Pilon "Debit Cards Overtake Credit Cards"
August 6, 2009, 12:56 PM ET

If the past two decades have been difficult for you, as a funeral director and funeral home owner, it was only preparation and training for the next decade. Americans were basically shy compared to how they will be as consumers. Whereas in the past they asked for better value, they will now demand it. The next decade will see funeral service continue to evolve:

- The tipping point that will change funeral service is not more people opting for cremation, but baby boomers choosing not to purchase pre-need cemetery property. With each death, a smaller percent of the population owns cemetery property. Certainly, many families continue to purchase at-need cemetery property, but fewer are choosing to purchase pre-need grave space. With the increasing cost of burial and popular consumerism challenging the value of memorials, there is less of an onus on cremation. In actuality, the tipping point has probably already occurred; it's just not visible yet because so many seniors own pre-need cemetery property.

- Consumers are demanding discounts. "Cash for clunkers" was a federal government funded rebate program. It was outstandingly successful from the perspective it brought buyers out of the woodwork. These consumers were driving the clunkers right up to the time they traded them in, meaning they represented viable transportation that would still be in use today had the government not provided the stimulus. The deal was too good to pass up, so they purchased new cars. Discounting, whether federally or business funded, has become the standard as retailers of all types look for new ways to advertise their lower prices. Funeral service will not be excluded from this bloodletting; discount funeral service will thrive during the next decade. Consider it this way; compare the number of high-end steak houses in a market to the number of lower-priced steak houses; all of the Cody's Road House Grills, Texas Long Horns, and the like to the number of Ruth Chris's, Fleming's and others. Lower-priced death care will represent the norm while the higher-end funeral homes, charging for and delivering full service, will be the exception. The majority of families will choose something less, while a few families will maintain the tradition. Look at the families you serve; where are they eating steak now? If there going to a family steak house, chances are they will be looking to reduce the cost of funeral service.

- Funeral businesses will seek special niches to elevate profits. Continuing the restaurant analogy, to compete with lower-priced competitors, restaurants create special dishes that are difficult for competitors to duplicate. Fondue is not offered by many restaurants, neither is bouillabaisse, paella, or osso bucco. These dishes demand special equipment and preparation procedures. To offer them a restaurant must serve enough volume to justify the labor invested. Because these dishes are uncommon restaurant faire, guests are willing to pay more at restaurants that offer them. The same applies to funeral services; consumers will be attracted to firms that offer the niche products others don't.

  - Green funerals and natural burial. If you think environmentalism is a fad, remember the federal government invested 3 billion dollars to get consumers to buy more fuel efficient vehicles. Try to think of another fad we the people have invested that much money in.

  - Reception rooms with catered food services.

- In contrast to over a century of tradition, ethnic division in funeral service will come to an end. Economic pressures will break down ethnic barriers in funeral service just as they have in every other industry. For years urban-based funeral homes have recognized their greatest competition for upwardly mobile African American business was the Caucasian-owned suburban funeral homes. Discounters serve an ethnically diverse clientele, as do historic cemeteries like Woodlawn, Spring Grove and others. Adding funeral homes on the grounds of cemeteries like Spring Grove, Mountain View Cemetery, and Cypress Lawn creates an ethnically diverse clientele for the funeral home. African American families prefer traditional services and have become such attractive business that Anglo-owned firms are beginning to direct their marketing efforts toward that community. This will cause some African American businesses to close as volume declines; but it will also teach Anglo-owned firms how funeral business was conducted generations ago when the Caucasian families were more church based and the clergy actually played an important role in the funeral service.

- Funeral businesses have never felt comfortable charging for facilities, preferring to load costs on merchandise instead. Certainly they have had to change as the FTC required cost breakdowns on price lists, so there are charges now for visitation rooms and chapels. But relatively few funeral homes are charging for use of reception rooms, and few if any are charging appropriately for cremation. A wonderful example of under charging for cremation is the comparison between the cemetery's charges for grave opening versus a funeral home's charges for cremation. A backhoe costs nearly the same as a crematory, but the cemetery charges $1195 for a grave opening versus a funeral home's charge of $250 for a wholesale cremation. Based upon this analogy, whole sale cremation should cost $1200, and retail should be $3500 to $5000 for the cremation alone. As the cremation rate approaches 50%, funeral homes will need to show some pricing courage and elevate the cost for cremation to a level that sustains their business model.

- Getting consumers to pay higher cremation prices will be a marketing challenge because there will always be low-end providers. Part of this challenge will be directing consumers' attention to the many cremation-based scandals over the past ten years. For many this will feel like airing dirty laundry, but until the consumer truly believes they get what they pay for with low-priced cremation, there will be no reason for them to pay more to an ethical service provider with fair prices.

- Another real issue is pre-need. For the past decade, most funeral homes have offered pre-paid services at a discounted price, either intentionally or unintentionally. Many funeral homes offer discounts from their current price lists, others simply fail to increase prices often enough causing pre-needs to be sold at a price below their true costs. In either event, by the time the death occurs, the trust or insurance contract is insufficient to match the firm's current prices.

  This raises the question as to whether pre-need should be sold with the understanding that the family's cost have been frozen. Instead of the funeral home taking the burden of rising costs, why not pass that onto the family by offering a choice of paying more now to assure no additional charges at the time of funeral, or pre-pay based upon current prices with the understanding that additional funds or other decisions might be necessary at time of death.

- Imported caskets are another pressing issue. Do Americans prefer domestic caskets, and if so, at what price point will they knowingly make a decision to use a lower cost imported product? Also, what are the real costs of imported caskets.

- Will technology enhance funeral home advertising? Social networking is proving successful in many industries, but what about one that serves the most senior segment of the population and when the ceremony occurs so quickly, compared to weddings and anniversaries?

Summary: The greatest news story of the year, even more important than the economy and wars, is the public's outcry at efforts to fundamentally change the health care system. Average citizens becoming violently angry at the policies they voted in only a year earlier. If there is any doubt we are looking at a changed consumer, one that knows what they want and is willing to demand it, angry town meetings should dispel the thought.

CHAPTER 2

A Change in Attitude

During the 90's many funeral home owners became complacent business people.

- They made acquisitions without due diligence.
- They delayed investments in facilities, or
- They stayed in the old neighborhood long after their customer base migrated to the suburbs.

Often, these decisions were made with the confidence that if their bet turned out badly, one of the acquisition companies would bail them out. Today, owners and managers are more conscientious about their decision-making and are apt to apply good management principles. Evidence of this is the elevated use of market research. When making a decision that can impact the rest of your working life, it's important to know as much about the risk your taking as possible. This includes understanding how a specific group of consumers select funeral homes.

Without research it is difficult for a business owner or practitioner to incorporate consumers' priorities in their decision-making simply because funeral home managers and owners have one set of priorities, consumers have another.

MANAGEMENT'S PRIORITIES	CONSUMERS' PRIORITIES
Facilities	Image/reputation
Products	Convenience
Inventory	Flexibility in services and prices
Staffing	Logistics

Based upon consumer research studies conducted by MKJ Marketing.

Certainly the issues considered important by management are expensive, and critical; but for many consumers they are the minimum expectations. Consumers just assume the structural elements of the business will present.

Consumers' priorities are intangible, and hard to measure. They are a mindset which either exists in the firm or doesn't. Sensitivity to consumers' priorities is the difference between a leading firm versus one of the available alternatives to the best. Not being responsive to consumers' priorities is the difference between being outstandingly successful and simply staying in business.

Funeral Home Design

Further evidence of the heightened sensitivity to the consumer is the design of new funeral homes. More emphasis is placed on how the consumer uses the building as opposed to how it serves the needs of staff and owners. Rooms to occupy children are included in the plans of most new buildings, just as are rooms for receptions following services.

With retirees living in downsized retirement community housing, it is impractical for family and friends to congregate at the home of the surviving spouse. Certainly, many families reserve banquet rooms at nearby restaurants, but that typically demands a larger meal (and expense) than many families can afford or want.

A reception room at the funeral home is convenient, and right sized for a casual reception. Since most consumers do not relate to a funeral home as an appropriate location to consume alcohol, having the reception at the funeral facility reduces the catering cost to the family while contributing to a more sober and less eventful reception.

More importantly, the introduction of food service at a funeral home opens a new profit stream. Funeral homes in Canada will often realize as much profit from food service as they do from casket sales.

Better Trained Staff

The greatest service a funeral home can offer is a well-informed arranger prepared to assist the family in arranging services meaningful to them. Research and practical experience have demonstrated the importance of effective listening and communication skills. Guiding families in the personalization of a funeral service stirs their creativity and is the foundation of a meaningful and profitable service.

Developing these skills in an experienced arranger can be far more challenging than training a recent mortuary school graduate. Most industries overcome a reluctance to change through the use of commissions. If funeral arrangers suffered financially when they arranged a minimal service, they would be more receptive to learning new arrangement and communication skills.

Advertising

The most visible change in the funeral home modus operandi is elevated visibility of advertising. The use of productive advertising is a factor of the changing communities. Although many communities remain stable, with little in and out mobility, there are fewer each year. As large cities sprawl they envelope small, rural communities which had changed little over decades. As the once sedentary community becomes the weekend haunt of suburban-landed gentry, funeral homes have found it is necessary to advertise to these new arrivals if they are to maintain their market share in the growing community.

Further, urban sprawl never goes unnoticed by the usually larger, city-based firms looking to grow. As such, the new opportunity typically brings new competition. The long established firm always starts out with the advantage, but can lose it to the newer, better-planned facilities with consumer-oriented floor plans and more effective advertising.

Another factor contributing to the greater use of advertising is the realization by small business owners in general that not all advertising is productive. In general, small business is more inclined to use paid media as opposed to novelty items (personalized rain hats, pens, combs, etc.) As media compete for the small businesses advertising, their rates become more affordable, particularly during difficult economic times such as the present.

Competing with "Dignity"

Casual surveys of independent funeral home owners revealed approximately one of ten have no familiarity with the strategy of affinity marketing. Just to assure a base of understanding, affinity marketing refers to cooperative efforts between two or more organizations to enhance the productivity of their individual marketing efforts. In funeral service, both large national corporations as well as individual funeral homes have approached employers and associations to offer pre-need and at-need services to employees and members, respectively.

Affinity marketing efforts elevate the productivity of traditional pre-need advertising efforts. A traditional pre-need direct mail piece is a far more productive lead generator when it includes a signed letter or statement from a national Commander, Grand Potentate, or corporate officer recommending the program.

The critical question regarding affinity marketing is whether the identification to an employer or association is greater than the relationship a family has with the funeral home that has served them in the past. Affinity marketing, as much as any marketing strategy in the past twenty years, will surely test the long held belief of many funeral home owners that "their families" belong to them and would never consider another firm.

Fortunately, to date, none of the affinity marketing programs have offered deep discounts. The costs involved in establishing the affinity relationships, the fees owed to the associations and related partners for their participation, have forced the prices to remain near or above those charged by competing firms. However, once the costs of establishing affinity relationships are recovered, and the various partners look for ways to increase volume, it is likely the price card will be played.

Competing with affinity marketing efforts is a matter of brand management and customer satisfaction. The more competitive a business, the more important it is for customers to be extremely satisfied.

Again referring to how owners look at their firms versus consumers; too often an owner's focus is on those elements the consumer considers as a given. Buying neighborhood houses to convert to parking is an expensive undertaking for any land-locked funeral home in a residential neighborhood. On the other hand, having sufficient parking is considered a given by many consumers.

Remodeling the ground floor to provide wheelchair access is expensive to do correctly, particularly when it also requires the addition of handicap restrooms. But for a business whose primary clientele is the elderly, these are not frills. Instead, they are the minimum expectations of a population accustomed to shopping at malls and Walmarts.

More than ever before it is critical funeral homes focus on what they can do to provide added value; to amaze their clientele with fresh, new ideas and to communicate these efforts in practice and in advertising.

Funeral service should study the local grocery store chains that have successfully competed against the far larger grocery store chains by doing the unexpected. The retail grocery business is extremely competitive and the national grocery chains are typically able to offer lower prices because of their volume buying capabilities. Nonetheless, in those situations where the local company has chosen to be different by truly meeting consumers' needs, they have been able to use the national companies' size against them. Large companies are not as responsive as a determined, family-owned business.

Local funeral homes must meet the challenge of affinity marketing by establishing themselves in the consumers' mind as so far superior, that even a "special deal" through an employer or association is considered an insufficient trade off.

Summary: The 1990's were an anomaly. Inflated stock values and a political environment that encouraged excess seemingly rewarded business owners for what has proven to be bad decision making. The sobriety of the first decade of the new millennium has marked a return of business as usual:

A battle for market share.

Concentration on profit margin and cash flow.

Keeping consumers' priorities as job one.

If it's any consolation, the return to reality extends far beyond just funeral service. Heck, even Major League Baseball and the players' union recognized the importance of their fans and avoided a strike.

CHAPTER 3

Funeral Service is Now a Fully Competitive Business

Michael Porter, the Harvard Professor that studies the elements of competition, defined a perfectly competitive environment in a *Harvard Business Review* article some years ago:

1. There is a constant threat of new competition in a perfectly competitive environment.
2. The customer is empowered to challenge prices, and to negotiate individual deals. (Many funeral homes have an active "no walk" policy, which is in effect, a response to consumers' most effective negotiating tactic; i.e., leaving one firm to go to another.)
3. Price increases are difficult to implement as shoppers have many options.
4. Competitors are constantly seeking new opportunities for investment as they prospect for better margins.
5. Vendors hold the stronger position in negotiating with manufacturers or retailers. Presently, the casket industry is in as much turmoil as the funeral homes they vend. However, the casket companies will ultimately right themselves, and the vendors will come to command their relationship with funeral homes.

Certainly, by this measure, funeral service is a very competitive environment, and has been for at least the past decade. All of the transition in the industry since 1990 can be attributed to the increasingly competitive environment that has evolved over this time.

Given the increasingly competitive environment, what should funeral home owners endeavor to accomplish? There will ultimately be a new kind of deathcare business; one that better addresses consumers' priorities than any of today's offerings. It will be different, and it will be better, which will make it profitable. What form will this new entity take? To divine that, let's look at the consumer's priorities compared to the elements the industry holds dear, with the object of defining a new deathcare business.

There is a new, popular business tome circulating through the airport bookstores entitled, *"Blue Ocean Culture"*, the premise of which is that businesses stuck in the red oceans of competition will inherently focus attention on the factors that define traditional competition within that industry as opposed to seeking blue oceans of opportunity by redefining their business to better meet consumers' priorities.

The process of redefining a business is one of comparing and contrasting the factors the consumer considers important with the factors the service providers consider important.

i.e., funeral homes and funeral home owners place significant importance on the following:

- Licensure
- Facilities
- Service
- Price
- Formality & tradition
- Clergy relationships
- Professionalism
- Quality merchandise
- Merchandising systems
- Vehicles
- Formal facilities

In contrast, the consumer, based upon present lifestyles, would suggest the following factors are important to them:

- Food service
- Casual facilities

- Convenience, in terms of location
- Convenience, in terms of one company providing all of their needs
- Individualization
- Take a look at the evolving marketing strategies and how they will impact the industry.

Consolidation

First it was family-owned funeral homes, then it was vendors. SCI consolidated disparate vendors, offering fluids, clothing, caskets, and insurance products. The effort proved a failure for that particular company, but vendor consolidation continues in the casket industry, and will likely expand to include vaults in the coming years.

The increasing cremation rate has caused the number of urn manufacturers and supply businesses to grow to ridiculous levels over and above the demand, consolidation will likely not occur to any significant degree in this segment of the industry simply because there are so many. Instead, small vendors will simply disappear.

Several years ago there was a spate of consolidation among pre-need insurance product providers as several of the larger players acquired a number of debit insurance companies from southern states, and folded them into their organization. This will likely prove inconsequential compared to the significant consolidation that will occur in that corner of the industry. It should be apparent to any casual observer that most funeral homes will never invest effort or resources into effective pre-need marketing. For most funeral homes, serving walk-in pre-need families is the extent of their interest. Only a third of the approximately 17,500 independent funeral homes nationally are actually productive with pre-need, and these firms hold such a strong negotiating position with the insurance companies, the insurers cannot even make a reasonable profit from the good producers. Look for the insurance companies to consolidate to the point where there are only three or four, and then watch them re-organize and re-structure their products to allow them to make a modest profit, at the expense of the funeral homes.

Creating a Strategy

What competitive concepts should the funeral home operator consider when thinking strategically? Five qualities have emerged as the most common characteristics of successful funeral firms. In the 14 years at my company, MKJ Marketing, has helped firms create business strategies using consumer attitude research.

In other words, one or more of the following five elements are present in funeral homes that are successful.

1. An image of flexibility in services and price.

Funeral directors typically think of service in terms of attention given to each family that selects the firm. Of course that is critical to long-term success, but the reality is most independent funeral homes provide a level of service consistent with their clientele's expectations. This negates attentive service as a competitive advantage.

The promotion of services not perceived to be available from other firms is another perspective. For the most part, flexibility in service and prices is not considered an image asset by most traditional funeral service providers. Advising the community of the availability of cremation services – not minimal or low-priced services – as an alternative to burial is an example of promoting flexibility. Similarly, promoting pre-need, aftercare, and other special services will attract some segment of the market.

In this era of market segmentation in funeral service, much of the challenge to traditional funeral firms is in niche products – services aimed at capturing a portion of the market that wants an alternative. Traditional funeral service competes best with discounters, combinations, and minimal cremation services by promoting flexibility.

Flexibility is also effective in competing with cemeteries that are selling funeral merchandise. The cemetery sales presentation is simply that funeral homes only offer expensive caskets and vaults. Because consumers are not well informed about funeral merchandise pricing, they can't see through the cemetery's sales pitch and thus too often yield to high pressure tactics. This sales approach will fail only when consumers truly believe funeral homes are flexible in price and service.

2. Superior facilities and/or convenience.

Quite often a successful firm is seen as having the most convenient location for a specific consumer base. Too often, the location of a new facility or branch is selected because it is convenient for everyone. However, consumers don't consider whether a location is convenient for everyone when they select a funeral home. They only consider what is convenient for them.

Branching is a strategy of providing convenience with an investment that is consistent with the opportunity. A well-planned, 100-call branch is far more profitable than a poorly placed facility doing 175 calls with a capacity for 350. A pin map analysis of a year's business will identify a population base sufficient to support a branch operation. Intelligent branching is a process of placing efficient facilities in a market area that is very convenient for an identifiable subgroup of the population.

A secondary benefit of opening branches is to preserve an opportunity by discouraging competitors. While total deaths in a growing community may be relatively low today, the death rate increases over time. Waiting to build leaves the area open to other competitors. An efficient branch is an opportunity to create an identity and build relationships. Later, when others enter the market, they do so at a significant disadvantage.

3. Consolidation.

Consolidation is an effective strategy to reduce incremental costs and increase efficiency. All independents should look at other funeral homes in the region to identify acquisition opportunities. Although the cost of an acquisition is high, if the national firms can justify the price, the cost should make sense to a firm in the same geographical area.

4. Promotion and advertising.

All other issues being relatively equal, there are many examples of ways effective promotion has proved to be a successful method of building volume. One reason effective funeral home advertising is so successful is because the majority of advertising is poor. Most funeral firms invest their limited advertising budgets in the wrong media, and their placement is unplanned and sporadic. Their ads often communicate points of little or no interest to the consumer.

A good example is name awareness advertising – 80% of consumers can name most of the viable funeral homes in their area, our research indicates, so additional name-awareness advertising is useless.

A better investment of an advertising budget would be to show the differences between competing firms. The effectiveness of promoting local ownership in competing with national firms is more apparent each month. Understanding the consumer's preference for family-operated funeral homes can be a factor determining the effectiveness of your advertising. Effective advertising is a complicated challenge for any manager. The most expensive advertising is that which accomplishes nothing; effective advertising can be the firm's most important investment.

5. Price.

The consumer is becoming increasingly value conscious. Because funeral homes typically are preoccupied with what their competitors down the street are doing, the industry as a whole has failed to communicate the value of the services it provides. This has created an opportunity for discounters and providers of minimal services. These low-cost alternatives have undermined consumer confidence in traditional funeral service by challenging the value of ceremony and facilities.

The discounter builds volume by providing a similar service at a lower price. When volume attains a sufficient level, the discounter adopts a full-service pricing structure. It is a time-tested strategy. The discounter is most vulnerable in the first 18 months. Once they have established a clientele, discounters are as stable as any other firm in the market, maybe more so.

Defending against discounters.

Rule 1. Lay the groundwork for your defense before the discounter arrives by promoting flexibility of services and prices, and by making prearrangements.

Rule 2. Never bring attention to the low-cost provider, either as an individual or as a group. A firm should increase its advertising, communicating its strengths, not the deficiencies of a competitor. Attacking a discounter will focus attention on the firm, and free promotion is important to the long-term success of an alternative provider.

Rule 3. Wait them out. Low-cost alternatives typically go that route because they don't have the financial resources for, or don't want to invest them in, a quality, convenient facility. If a discounter fails to get free publicity, it is forced to invest heavily in promotion. Because the discounter depends on volume to succeed, it must pull business from a very large area and advertising can be quite expensive. A discount firm should expect to invest $50,000 in advertising each year until it establishes a clientele. If business does not come early, a discounter can encounter cash flow problems.

Offering low-cost traditional packages, promoting flexibility, and crowding out the discounter's self-promotion with your own messages will complicate their efforts at building a business.

In Summary: Funeral service is midway through a complete transition to a retail-oriented, fully-competitive business. The business concepts that succeed are those consistent with the social trends that contribute to a society's collective opinions. Too often, funeral home owners look to their firm's long past for answers to challenges never before faced. Too often, the answer divined from the past is to do nothing. This creates opportunities for alternative service and merchandise providers.

Strategic planning is a process in which management attempts to weigh the assets and liabilities of each player in a market, whether it is a market in which the firm presently competes or one it is considering. If a business, or a concept, can cite no strategic advantage, it is likely to fail. Most markets, though, provide an opportunity for a new competitor with well-laid plans.

CHAPTER 4

Preparing for Another Round of Acquisition

One reason acquisition has failed as a strategy for many funeral home operators, both large and small, is that the acquisitions were made with the assumption that competition within the industry would continue to be soft and compliant. But such has not been the case, and is certainly not the case now. We have all witnessed the carnage when an absentee owner competes with local owners.

Many of the most successful funeral businesses sold in the 1990's simply because the multiples being offered were so great, it seemed the intelligent decision and for many it worked out well. Because the multiples paid for funeral homes this time around will not be great enough to tempt a well-managed funeral business owner to sell (well managed in terms of profit and having a succession plan in place).The quality firms will be acquirers this time around instead of sellers. Sellers this time around will fall into two types: those without a succession plan, and marginal firms that can no longer compete.

Realizing it's going to be tough competition, what are the factors the intelligent acquirer should consider before he commits to a new mortgage for the right to compete in a new market?

> First, acquire in markets with limited competition: When an outsider acquires in a market with multiple family-owned funeral homes, business tends to shift to the other locally-owned businesses. Remember this, success in the funeral business isn't about doing everything right – it's about relationships. Very bad locally-owned businesses will do well against very well-run businesses owned by an out of town company simply "because the families that used to go to their best friend for funerals, will now go to their second best friend". *(Quote attributed to Paul Henney, Henney Family Services.)*

So, we want to buy in small towns where there is little competition, preferably in communities where at least one of the competitors is owned by a national or regional consolidator.

Or, we want to acquire in small towns where there are little or no other funeral homes, and I mean really small towns, some as small as 2000 people, serving counties of 10,000, where there is only one funeral home. Cremation is minimal, and services are traditional, even when cremation is selected.

Second, realize up front that success depends upon a good manager. If we learned anything from the acquisition of the 1990's, former owners make lousy managers. If they wanted to run a business, they wouldn't have sold. Most of the sellers were tired, and wanted to retire; not work harder for a regional manager.

What does it mean to be a good manager? They need to focus on the community, not the funeral home. A good manager realizes his competitive disadvantage from the beginning and mobilizes his efforts to create relationships. This is accomplished by hiring well-known part-timers and initiating programs that get the staff involved with the public.

Third, acquire businesses that are clearly superior in some discernible way, such as combinations, discounters, superior facilities in terms of parking or special features such as reception rooms, children's rooms, or location.

Fourth, don't operate an acquired firm on a budget; operate it as if it is the only business you own. Budgets are a formula for failure. Well-run family businesses do whatever is necessary to make their business successful, even if it means suffering a cut in salary for a few months to improve their competitive position. But these same people will make an acquisition in another community, never visit the town after the deal is made, and fail to make the necessary investments to make their acquisition successful, such as advertising and staff training.

Fifth, when scrutinizing acquisition candidates, select the firms that are clearly superior or make the necessary investment to make it clearly superior. Stewart Enterprises fared better in the 1990's than other acquisition companies because they had a value-added philosophy; they acquired cemeteries and made them into combinations, then acquired free-standing funeral homes in the same markets to operate as branches. They improved their competitive position by investing in the properties.

Being clearly superior is not exclusive to facilities. Acquirers can be clearly superior by investing in marketing concepts and training. It is safe to assume most funeral directors in the country could be made better with training. Changes in society have made arranging a funeral much more difficult. Constructive arrangement skills are not taught in mortuary school, and even if they were, most of the licensed funeral directors in the country have been practicing so many years, they did not benefit from new curriculum.

Arrangers need sales tools to be effective; the consumer is not aware of all of the options available to them in personalization and memorials. Good arrangers have tools at their disposal that help to make them more effective communicators; tools that allow the consumer to see why they should invest in a limo versus driving their own cars, what a piper musical program is and how dove releases, butterfly releases, and balloon releases make a graveside service more memorable.

Consolidation in death care is inevitable, including casket companies, vault companies, pre-need insurance companies, and operators. Bankruptcy is not. The corporate turmoil of the past five years was not so much a factor of consolidation as it was buyers making buying decisions instead of operational decisions. Many independent operators would have benefited from challenging themselves as to how they were going to compete in a market before they decided to make an acquisition.

The Disappearing Funeral Home Manager

It is interesting to observe how different funeral businesses organize for expansion. Early on, most firms would assign a manager to be the primary contact at new facilities. This individual was responsible for building maintenance, public relations, and quality control within his domain. In recent years it has been interesting how many independent firms are moving away from funeral home managers, opting instead to assign funeral directors to individual events and dispatching them from a central office. As such, the individual the family meets with initially may not even be working the day of the visitation or funeral. While this practice might appear expeditious from the perspective of manpower utilization, it is very unproductive from a marketing perspective.

Dan Stevens, former independent funeral home owner, and current Carriage Enterprises executive, talks convincingly that relationships, not superior service, create satisfied customers and keep them loyal. Constructive relationships can only be created through a consistent and stable workforce. Consumers want to identify with their funeral director; it is for this reason the second most common reason for preferring a funeral home is knowing a staff member. The most common reason is past experience with the firm, from which a personal relationship was very likely created, and contributed to the consumer's loyalty.

Just as a funeral home's success in pre-need is typically determined by the availability of a good counselor, successful expansion is also dependent upon the presence of a good manager. Truly any decisions to expand should be based upon the availability of a trusted individual that can make the new facility a success.

CHAPTER 5

Marketing Leadership

Funeral service, indeed, the entire death care industry is in a crisis. New competitors are entering every facet of the business, including caskets from third world countries, churches, country clubs and universities announcing columbarium niches projects, Hilton Hotels promoting funeral services at their facilities, the Catholic Church operating their own funeral homes in Oakland and Denver and selling pre-need funerals in Pittsburgh. The only segment in the industry without new competition is the burial vault business, and it is experiencing hard times from the growth in cremation. The crisis is taking its toll on the industry as desperate funeral home and cemetery owners make decisions that place their business, even their life, in jeopardy. Notice the proliferation of the pre-need scandals in both the cemetery and funeral home businesses over the past year. Every month or so another case surfaces where an owner filed false death certificates or ransacked a cemetery's perpetual care fund.

Not all of these challenges have ready solutions, but it is important to remember from crisis comes opportunity. Remember the gas crisis in the 1970's; it caused significant hardship on consumers, challenged the American auto companies, and drove major airlines into bankruptcy. But from this upheaval the Japanese auto companies got a foothold in the U.S. market by producing fuel efficient, quality small cars, and a new breed of airlines was introduced by "People's Express," which led to Southwest Airlines, ATA, JetBlue and others. During crisis, companies willing to do things differently can establish new ways of doing business and capture market share.

Marketing is any activity an enterprise engages in to create new business or retain business.

There is a small Greek lunch restaurant near our offices that seats about 25 people, well known for their Greek salads and gyros. It's run by a Greek man and his family. Average check is about $12.50. The owner hand picks the tomatoes every morning and takes great pride in his food quality. Stavros greets each customer from behind the counter, and Laura asks about the kids.

Also in Tampa is a nationally recognized local steakhouse known for the most diverse wine cellar in the U.S. The restaurant serves hundreds of diners every night with an average check around $60.00. Fish swim in a large tank on the roof, and a few are brought down to a smaller tank located in the kitchen to be served that day. All the vegetables are grown organically on a farm operated by the restaurant. Wait persons train for six months at minimum wage before they are allowed to address a customer. Patrons are invited on kitchen and wine cellar tours after dinner, as they segue to the separate dessert room.

Both establishments serve food and drinks, and accept tips, but that's where the similarities end. There are restaurants like these two in nearly every city in the country. No one would walk into Stavros' expecting a bottle of rare wine, and no one would expect to see Bern in the foyer of his 25,000 sq. ft. building. We are willing to pay $60 average at Bern's and expect to be wowed. No one is willing to pay $60 for a gyro and iced tea, no matter how interested Laura is in the kids.

Funeral home businesses in the U.S. range from 35 cases annually to 25,000 plus. At the small volume facilities, the owner and family are intimately involved in serving clients. They collect the remains, meet with the survivors, prepare the body, print the memorial cards, coordinate and arrange personalization, and greet visitors at the door. The average price of their services is very competitive with other funeral homes in the market, but typically less than national competitors and large independent firms.

At the large-volume firms, with call volumes of 600 and up; the funeral home arranges for first call, a funeral director meets with the family to make arrangements, the body is prepared, personalization is arranged, and someone holds the door for visitors. Typically, the owner or member of the owner's family does not meet the client. Typically the fees are somewhat higher than the small-volume competitors, but the services provided, even the facilities, are often not very different, and sometimes not as nice as the smaller volume competitors.

Focus groups recently conducted for a leading, Mountain zone death care company raised some interesting comments from the respondents. When asked what a funeral home could do to be superior, someone in each group explained the benefits and advantages of the working with the same funeral director throughout the funeral process. Nearly all small-volume firms accomplish this simply because there is no one else to assign to the family. But many large-volume firms, for the sake of scheduling and efficiency, hand families off from one director to another. If consumers consider having a single contact person at the funeral home as a priority, then the smaller firms actually provide a higher standard of service than do their higher-priced competitors.

Large-volume funeral home owners grouse openly about not being able to gain volume, which begs the question, "What do the large firms do to make themselves' more competitive?" Restaurants, hotels, even automobile companies, differentiate their products and prices. A Mitsubishi is less expensive than the very popular Toyota, and no one would confuse a Lexus with a Kia. Bern's Steakhouse in Tampa does not "need" to grow their own vegetables, or offer 30 different varieties of caviar or have the nation's most diverse wine selection, but all of these efforts combine to make them superior to Ruth's Chris, Fleming's, The Capital Grille and other national companies. Do any of these national companies conduct kitchen and wine cellar tours to raise the customers' appreciation for their standard of excellence?

What's missing in death care is the marketing leadership one would expect from the largest funeral companies. In fact, it's the largest companies (the corporations included) that institutionalize the traditional service within their operations. Where is the "out of the box" thinking that would allow a discerning consumer to justify a premium price to be wowed? Funeral homes have depended on vendors to innovate for so long, current owner operators really don't know how. What they have learned is how to make accounting decisions as opposed to marketing decisions.

To establish excellence; excellence must be defined, and by who's definition? Is Bern's an excellent restaurant by the standards set by other restaurateurs or by consumers' standards? Perhaps both; but it is more important to meet the consumers' standards than that of other funeral directors.

NFDA's Pursuit of Excellence is an excellent program at measuring excellence as defined by the funeral profession. Awards are based upon pointless public relations such as aftercare, which consumers' have demonstrated a complete lack of interest, instead of pre-need which has generated billions of dollars in sales, or owning and operating crematories, or offering reception room services, all of which meet consumer-based needs. Apparently, the fact that these efforts also generate profit disqualifies them as a basis of excellence. Any wonder why so many funeral homes are in financial jeopardy; the profession's standard for excellence is based upon providing unnecessary services that generate cost instead of profit.

The acquisition companies made a fundamental error in the 1990's by not promoting the fact that they were national companies; instead they attempted "stealth" acquisitions which the local competitors took advantage of. Many of the large, independent firms are committing a similar mistake now. They have lost sight of the priorities established by the earlier generations that managed their family businesses. Instead of separating themselves from the pack in their local markets, they manage their businesses to maximize short-term profit instead of investing to improve their long competitive position.

And the cemeteries are even worse. With the cremation rate growing annually, very few cemeteries have made a sincere effort to educate the consumer in cremation memorialization; less than 5% of the population is familiar with the term "columbarium" or know that they can bury cremated remains. Increasingly country clubs, universities, churches and other institutions are creating memorialization options for cremation families. Certainly, fundamental advertising to educate consumers will not generate cash flow as quickly as a free veteran's space direct mail advertisement, but if sustained, it will create future demand for cemetery products.

Just as most cities have a hotel or restaurant that is clearly superior, not just in that market, but even comparable to other cities; some mid-sized firms are achieving the standard of "clearly superior." In Rochester, NY, the Bartolemeo-Perroto Funeral Home operates clearly superior facilities for that particular market; in fact, it may be the finest funeral facility in upstate New York. Curlew Hills Memorial Gardens in Clearwater, FL is an excellently maintained and marketed cemetery, in a very tough cemetery market. Money & King Funeral Home in McLean, VA offers superior facilities in a market where property values preclude most companies from providing such extravagance as off-street parking. Sure, they could sell the building for property value, but instead they have established a standard of service (in terms of convenience and facilities) competitors cannot approach. Moloney Funeral Home on Long Island, NY and Anderson-McQueen in St. Petersburg, FL provide first-rate facilities, enhanced by separate facilities specifically for cremation families.

The reality is that most of death care has placed innovation at a very low priority level. Vendors, through desperation to spark the consumers' interest have invested significantly to create new products, both in personalization and in the various containers (caskets, vaults and urns), and many funeral homes have attempted to incorporate these product innovations in their businesses. But there is far more attention being paid by the larger funeral companies to lower prices with Chinese caskets than to offer innovative products being created by domestic companies. Funeral directors have consistently, over many years, recommended sealing burial vaults developed in the 1960's as opposed to espousing the advantages of the more recently designed, metal lined vaults. Any wonder why educated consumers view funeral services as archaic?

How many funeral firms offer live music as an option in their "best" package; or hors d'oeuvres, valet parking, or child care? Concierge service is catching on, and that's good, but how many are firms offer a concierge service and how prepared are they to solve a family's problems?

Facility design has improved remarkably in recent years with new funeral homes combining home-like comforts with institutional conveniences. But the majority of the nation's funeral facilities remain converted old homes with too many steps, small rooms and chapels instead of reception rooms.

Minimum service cremation societies should have been a flash in the pan as funeral homes transitioned with the growing popularity of cremation versus burial. But instead, minimal service providers have gained a foothold in many markets taking hundreds of calls from traditional service providers. We, as an industry, should take advantage of the publicity gained from the various cremation scandals to explain the difference between minimal providers and professionally-operated funeral homes. Laws in states like Michigan, New York, and others should be changed to encourage funeral homes to install on-site crematories. Notice how many restaurants have open kitchens that allow diners to observe the cook staff. Consumers like to see what's going on, and appreciate being able to observe the cremation process.

Summary: K-Mart recently announced that the giant retailer, in an effort to attract higher income shoppers, is introducing a line of organic foods, including dairy, meat, pastas, etc. K-Mart became the world's largest employer and retailer by providing low-priced goods manufactured in China to America's middle income families.

Will higher income families more accustomed to the wide aisles and gentile environment of the "fresh market" visit K-Mart's cavernous and claustrophobic big boxes; maybe, probably not, but that's not a reason not to try. Businesses and industries are either innovative by nature, looking for new opportunities in every niche, or they're not. Businesses in competitive industries are typically the most innovative, and no industry is more competitive than discount retailing. However, with Internet caskets, cremation societies, discount funeral homes, and a declining death rate, the death care industry is very competitive.

Nonetheless, funeral homes and funeral practitioners are reticent to introduce packages of services that allow families to custom create their family's ceremony, instead offering a choice between a standard traditional service or a price competitive minimal cremation service. Cemeteries focus their attention on the declining burial market while churches, golf courses, universities and other institutions offer creative columbarium options. The question death care should be asking itself is, how long will the American consumer give us to get this right?

CHAPTER 6

Marketing Priorities

Many articles discussing marketing, whether in the funeral business or any other industry, begin with a definition of marketing as encompassing every activity within the business, not just the sales and advertising functions. Yet, most people continue to use the terms marketing and advertising synonymously. Simply put, anything your company does to generate new business or to hold customers is marketing; new buildings, pricing, employee training, sales tools, advertising, all fall under marketing.

Many death care industry businesses, including vendors, are in desperate need of new marketing plans, and it has little to do with advertising. Those death care industry businesses suffering from high overhead and shrinking margins, which include most of the funeral homes in the U.S., find themselves in their precarious positions because their present marketing plans are failing. Even if their advertising was more effective, these businesses would remain in a precarious position simply because their present plan of pursuing additional volume at any cost is not viable at a time when many of these services are provided at a loss.

For this reason, we should be shifting our attention away from advertising for the moment, and address issues of merchandising and pricing, integral aspects of a comprehensive marketing strategy. Just as an illustration, let's begin with caskets. Casket companies have arguably provided the industry with the highest level of merchandising support in the death care industry. Nonetheless, they consistently violate the most basic rule of merchandising: A product's more popular features should be reserved for the highest priced models. Everyone in the industry knows pink and blue are the two most popular colors for caskets. We also know that corner pieces, head panel embroideries, and other structural features (such as the drawers) are very popular. But instead of reserving these features for our highest priced units, they are (for the most part) available from the top to the near bottom of the line. Is it any wonder the public has difficulty seeing the value in higher priced units?

Instead of pricing units based upon popular features, casket pricing reflects the price of the materials used in creating the casket. Certainly copper and bronze are more expensive materials than steel, and mahogany is more rare and expensive than oak and pine; but 90% of American consumers really don't care what the casket is made of. They simply want an attractive, well-built piece of furniture with special features, such as the interchangeable corners, interiors that can be personalized, and their loved one's favorite color, and they would be willing to pay for the features they want.

Applying that same mentality to the funeral homes, why do funeral homes include all of their services in their basic package, thus depriving the family an opportunity to move up? More importantly, we take away the opportunity to make a decision; choosing the package that best serves their needs. NOTICE TO INDUSTRY: Consumers like choices.

Funeral homes should learn, as hotels have, that superior profits can only be generated by selling services, not merchandise. As funeral merchandise (caskets, vaults, and urns) become more available from alternative sources, such as retail outlets and the internet, it will be increasingly difficult to realize a reasonable profit from the sale of these products. Even worse, cremation families will increasingly argue they have no need for a casket or vault.

Profiting from services should be fundamental to the funeral business; why else would funeral homes operate large facilities with rooms appropriate for large gatherings of people. Certainly, very few funeral homes have anywhere near enough volume to simply operate as a furniture store; but they do serve enough families to profit as an event venue, utilizing their buildings, yet almost no funeral home effectively merchandises their services. Instead of incorporating graphics and other sales aids to assist arrangers in making effective arrangements, the funeral homes operate under the assumption that the consuming public is fully aware of all of their options, and will simply tell the arranger what they want.

Pre-need lead generation is based upon advertising concepts developed around the 1950's lifestyle when mom stayed home with the children, seniors lived with their children, before answering machines and e-mail. Cemetery direct mail advertising in the 1950's generated fifty times the results of direct mail today, at a time when postage was just pennies as opposed to $.39 a piece. The cost of getting a direct mail piece delivered is over $.40 a piece, including mailing lists and handling, and this is before the piece is created and printed. Every knowledgeable pre-need marketer in the business knows informative consumer seminars, family follow-up and public relations efforts generate far better quality leads, at a fraction of the cost. Nonetheless, the industry led by the pre-need insurance companies, continues to flood the nation with direct mail letters.

Incorporating the consumers' priorities in your marketing plan:

The popular business book, *"Blue Ocean Strategy"* discusses the concept that all industries operate under certain basic assumptions, which contributes to every company within an industry looking very much like all of the others. With such similarity, the only differentiation is the issue of price. The ongoing consolidation of the casket companies would be the anticipated corporate response to a declining market. Instead of creating a line of products in line with consumer's priorities, the priority is to reduce overhead costs per units, selling the products the industry has become accustomed to. As much as we would all prefer to sell American-made products, following this course to the ultimate conclusion will require funeral homes to offer lower-priced caskets manufactured outside the U.S. in order to get casket prices low enough that consumers can afford the higher-profit funeral home services, the funeral homes will have to sell to remain viable.

An objective analysis of the industries' priorities, based upon the similarities from funeral home to funeral home, would suggest that the industry places importance on the following items in descending order:

1. Service
2. Large facilities
3. Vehicles
4. Clergy
5. Formality
6. Aftercare

Suggesting "service" is a misplaced priority is tantamount to heresy, but the reality is most consumers are unable to evaluate a funeral home based upon services provided simply because they visit funeral homes too seldom to make comparisons. Further, when they are visiting a funeral home, they are so overwhelmed by the loss of their friend, the family's grief, and the realization of their own mortality, they cannot remember the color of the casket, let alone the quality of service provided.

Consider for a moment the lunacy of trading in a six to ten year old hearse with 15,000 miles on it in order to incur debt for a new vehicle. It is incomprehensible that anyone would believe consumers would select a funeral home based upon the age of the hearse. Funeral homes maintain their vehicles beautifully just to sell them before reaching mid-life. Those funds could be much better invested into a reception room that allows families to socialize following a funeral or equipment to create video tributes the family would consider a keepsake for generations.

Research indicates fewer than 5% of individuals would consult a clergy to recommend a funeral home, yet an immeasurable amount of time and money invested in church bulletins and contributions, are invested in influencing the clergy. The reality is churched families are very familiar with their funeral home options, and most people without a funeral home preference do not attend church on a regular basis. Besides, Episcopalians, Presbyterians, and some Methodists encourage their parishioners to minimize funeral services or to let the church handle the affair.

Examining the factors that consumers consider important when selecting a funeral home, we find issues that offer more tangible benefits. As consumers ourselves, we can understand why a consumer would be more inclined to contact a funeral home where they know a staff member or one that offered more convenience.

- Past experience 53%
- Knowing a staff member 18%
- Location 18%
- Price 1%

But instead of building more, smaller funeral homes, the industry persists in building large facilities strategically located to be the most convenient to a very large population instead of multiple, smaller buildings that are very convenient to specific populations. Families want a convenient funeral home to them and their friends, not one that is conveniently located between two fair-sized cities.

How many funeral homes include in their promotional budget, funds for building the community's awareness of their staff? As the second most volunteered reason for selecting a funeral home, building familiarity with staff members should be the most important promotional priority.

Summary: Reviewing funeral service from the consumer's perspective we find that funeral businesses, just like businesses in most other industries, focus resources in factors that deliver little in the way of customer value. Look at the opportunity realized by companies in other industries when they realized the industry modus operandi was diametrically opposite consumers' priorities.

For generations, roadside motels all included restaurants and lounges, even after the interstate system was created and hotels and restaurants began to build around the exits. Even though the restaurants and lounges consistently lost money, they were included in every motel until Hampton Inns ignored the well-defined norm and opened facilities that offered only sleeping rooms with a free continental breakfast. For years, Hampton Inns enjoyed a temporary, legal monopoly on a popular concept until competitors opened.

Operating differently would allow a funeral home to offer better value and a more rewarding service to families, in addition to building relationships with new families that will return in the future, even though other funeral homes will ultimately attempt to copy the leader's success.

The point being, most funeral homes are suffering badly from shrinking margins, and looking for solutions in the well-worn business practices that brought us to our present state of affairs. Marketing plans are the vehicles companies use to define their fundamental concepts. Developing a new strategy, or "marketing plan" that focuses on the consumer might result in discovering more profitable ways of operating funeral businesses and return the leaders to more comfortable profits.

CHAPTER 7

Funeral Home Advertising

Dr. Roger Blackwell, a nationally recognized marketing consultant, conducted return on Investment seminars for funeral home owners in the 1970's and early 80's. The objective of the seminars was to demonstrate the true cost of providing a funeral service. Because most family-owned funeral homes operated with little or no cost for their facilities, their charges for their services were far lower than they should have been. Simply put, their charges were based upon their out-of-pocket cost of providing a service, not their real cost since they did not include a charge for facilities. During that period it was common practice to load the cost on the casket.

The message of the ROI seminars was to charge based upon the real cost of providing a service, including charges for the facility. The theory was that someday it would be necessary to replace facilities and it may not be possible to pass all of the new, higher operating costs onto the consumer at that time.

Now, in the new millennium, Dr. Blackwell's seminars seem prophetic. Large corporations are saddled with staggering debt loads, but so are many family-operated firms. Without large corporations to acquire their funeral homes, owners approaching retirement turn to family members and employees to allow them to "cash out." Acquiring a successful family business requires a mortgage, perhaps the firm's first mortgage in generations.

There are new funeral homes sprouting up to compete with the national corporations, many of which are family members of individuals who sold the family business in the past decade. Because the stock taken in lieu of cash at the time of the sale is worth only a fraction of what it was at the time of the sale, the family must rely on bank financing to buy back the family business or to start a new business.

Many family firms are expanding by acquiring depleted businesses from the national corporations as they spin-off exhausted facilities they can no longer afford to maintain.

All of these scenarios contribute to a new reality in funeral service: there is simply not as much disposable cash in the industry as there once was. Instead of operating debt free, more owners than ever before find themselves sending a check to the bank each month. What impact does this have on the industry?

Most visibly, for many firms, it means needed repairs and remodeling are being delayed. Visitation rooms and chapels look tired, they need remodeling in order to keep up with consumers' changing expectations. Also, contemporary merchandising programs are not being implemented as quickly as they should. Casket selection rooms are not being remodeled as they would have been without the debt load. Vault displays are from another era. Urn selections are not as large as they should be.

All of these factors will contribute to an already growing consumer consensus that funeral service is out of date. If consumers question the relevance of the funeral, they will not be as likely to spend a little more to make the event "just right." With profit margins already a little tight and shrinking, it is not a good time to pull back on merchandising efforts.

Whenever economic trends turn down, whether in an industry or for the economy in general, there is an immediate knee jerk reaction to rein in advertising costs. Companies often go to their advertising budgets, hatchets in hand, to reduce costs and increase available cash. Rolling back ad budgets is simple and quick. Simple, quick and dangerous. What seems like prudence can endanger a company's very future.

During these times it is important to remember, "As advertising goes, so goes the company." The usual justification for cutting ad spending is to protect the "bottom line." However, studies show that companies that curtail their promotional programs realize no greater short-term returns on investment than their competitors who do not. More significantly, the companies that remain aggressive gain market share from their "prudent" competitors, thus securing an advantage that may never be made up. And, ultimately, market share shows up on the bottom line.

When a company sharply cuts advertising, its brand can suffer "memory decay," often with amazing speed. Worse, if competitors remain aggressive, a company and its products can lose mind share as well as market share; and so the vicious circle begins.

The cost of re-introducing a brand name is far greater than maintaining visibility.

Again, this is particularly true in funeral service where families are inclined to patronize a firm with positive momentum. If the past decade has taught us anything, it's that the greatest challenge in funeral service is reversing a slide. Once the public has branded a funeral home as "the one people use to go to," volume begins to drop quickly and it can take years to reverse.

Research proves that positive feelings toward a brand are directly related to the number of advertising exposures. The more people are exposed to your advertising, the more they will like your product and buy your product. This is particularly true in funeral service; 80% of consumers think all funeral homes are the same. The cumulative effect of a repetitive message is to establish the perception in the consumer's mind that one firm, your firm, is different and better.

Cutting advertising budgets can undermine the value of a business. With so many changes in ownership and staffing over the past ten years, the consumer often times has difficulty maintaining an accurate perspective of their various funeral home options. This process is made even more difficult when the line of communication is severed.

Ask yourself this question, *"How will your firm improve its position in the market without advertising and merchandising?"* Invisibility can be fatal. In most communities, one funeral home stands out as a market leader. Leaders prosper when competitors are in transition. The greater the leader's success during the transition period, the longer it will take the weaker firms to catch up. Perhaps they never will. The effect of high operating costs, shrinking profit margins, and declining market share can combine to cause another business phenomena heretofore uncommon in funeral service. Bankruptcy.

Reaching Baby Boomers

Death care has been planning and preparing for the baby boomer to age for twenty years. Many individual funeral homes have attempted to reach the extremely large baby boomer generation with pre-need over this period, with no success. Surprisingly, now that the baby boomers are actually attaining an age when they would be receptive to funeral home advertising, few funeral homes are making an effort to build credibility with these aging adults. Instead we prefer to direct our promotion to the oldest segment of society because we believe we have a better understanding of the WWII generation.

As the baby boomer generation turns 55, they are dealing almost daily with aging parents. Watching out for a parent is no longer academic; now it's reality. This generation of seniors, unlike previous generations, is open to listening, even soliciting their children's advice in all matters. Whether home electronics, financial investments, or funeral home selection, baby boomers are making the choices.

Baby boomers are the Walmart generation; they have learned to buy brand names at outlet malls, big box stores, even consignment. From the baby boomer perspective, all funeral homes are the same, and like any other commodity, it can be discounted.

Baby boomers are also value conscious. This generation has made "moving up" in quality an obsession. If something is good, something else is better, and baby boomers want better.

Demonstrating that your funeral home offers a quality difference is an objective of your advertising; which raises the question, "how do we reach the baby boomer?" American Demographics, an authoritative journal on consumer behavior addresses this issue often as baby boomers continue to be the driving force in all retail buying. Research study after study points to cable television as the most productive media for reaching baby boomers. The adjacent chart indicates that cable television viewing has increased 47% as broadcast television has increased only 10%, and newspaper readership has actually declined 5% between 1997 and 2002.

During that same period, consumer Internet use has increased 492%. Although use of the Internet by seniors is still minimal, baby boomers prefer the Internet to shopping by telephone or physically visiting facilities.

In the same study, 81.8% of consumers surveyed indicated they believe television commercials are more effective than advertising on any other media.

MKJ Marketing offers over fifty television advertising campaigns, more than ten of which were developed specifically to reach baby boomers. Each campaign includes support newspaper and radio advertisements.

Most funeral home owners are surprised when they learn how affordable cable advertising can be. Typically, clients run twenty to thirty television advertisements for the cost of a single newspaper ad. Allow an MKJ Marketing Advisor to collect cable rates from your local service.

Research conducted by MKJ Marketing in advance of creating the new "Price Competition" and "Value" campaigns suggests baby boomer adults are a major contributing factor in a family's choice of a discount funeral home.

It's for this reason, two of the advertisements feature a baby boomer spokesperson relating how "discounts are good when buying a toaster, but not when selecting a funeral home."

Cable TV Advertising: More Important Than Ever

In doing annual plans for clients throughout the country, one medium stands out as consistently yielding results over the long term *(and in some cases, the short term)* for funeral homes: advertising on cable networks such as CNN, LIFETIME, TNT, DISCOVERY, ARTS & ENTERTAINMENT, etc.

Cable television advertising has many unique attributes that make it ideal for funeral service:

Image and Credibility. Television is still the most results-oriented media due in large part because it involves sight, sound and motion; giving it more opportunity to capture the viewer's attention than radio (sound only) or newspaper (sight only). How is this an advantage? Let's say you're watching a cable program and it breaks for a commercial. Rather than watching, you start to read the paper, but suddenly you hear something (either music or voice) that draws your attention, then you find yourself watching the ad because the sight and motion continue to hold your attention.

Greater Opportunity for Creative Expression. Again, because television appeals to more senses, there are more ways to creatively capture consumers' attention while still presenting an appropriate professional message.

Low Cost. Per spot costs throughout the United States to air one 30-second advertisement on cable television between the hours of 6:OO AM and 12 midnight, range from $7 to $15 on average. For most markets, this means you can air 21 times in one week on cable for the same or less as running just one display newspaper ad. Because rates are based upon the number of subscribers, cable television always represents a good value; the only question is whether all of the households within the cable service area are viable prospects to employ your funeral firm's services. MKJ can assist you in making this determination by obtaining cable rates for the communities your funeral home services.

Name Awareness. Consumers without a specific funeral home preference will typically select the one whose name comes to mind first. This is especially true for those families who are new to an area and are not familiar with their funeral home options. Name awareness in general can be increased in addition to promoting a specific message such as pre-need, flexible services, facilities, etc.

Target Audience. Nearly 70% of all households subscribe to their local cable service. Subscribers tend to have a longer residency in a given area as well as a stable household income. This same demographic group represents premium funeral home business. With mature women playing an important role in at-need funeral home selections (70% of women will be widowed) and pre-need funeral home selections (80% of pre-need leads come from women age 55 plus); cable television offers networks with programming appropriate for funeral home advertising that attract this large female base.

Not only do they target the appropriate demographic group, but cable also targets the appropriate geographic group. Most cable systems cover a much smaller geographic area than broadcast TV (i.e., ABC, CBS, NBC), which is ideal for the funeral home market. This is also why it is so much more affordable than broadcast and results in less waste.

Cable Television Makes Other Advertising More Productive. Use cable TV to promote your Web site, open house, holiday programs and other special services. Airing spots in conjunction with a direct mail campaign will generally increase your response rate by about 50%. This is because the consumer sees the ad on TV and then has the message reinforced when they receive the piece in the mail. This is why many national advertisers will employ celebrities for television advertisements, then feature their picture on a subsequent direct mail piece.

Although cable is ideal for funeral service, there are keys to assure your campaign is most productive:

The Advertisements Must Meet the Viewer's Expectations for Quality, Creative Advertising.

On average, an advertiser will invest fifteen to twenty times more money to run an advertisement than they will in producing or purchasing an advertisement. It costs no more to run a good advertisement than it does to run an ineffective, poorly produced advertisement.

The most important factor in selecting a funeral is reputation, more important than facilities, services or prices. Without a good public image, there is nothing a funeral firm can do to significantly increase volume and profitability. Television advertising has the potential to enhance image more than any other advertising media, but the advertisements must meet the consumers' standards for creativity and production. Viewers don't have dual standards for advertising; national advertisements have established the standard for quality advertising. If your advertising does not meet that standard, viewers simply use their remote controls to find something more interesting. Funeral home advertising must be consumer-oriented, employ professional actors and actresses presenting creative messages that can impact the viewer's decision making process. Film, rather than videotape, projects a quality image, just as does the appropriate music, scripts and voice talent.

Low cost, poorly produced television advertisements cause consumers to judge your business as below their standards. After all, people have funerals to pay a tribute to a deceased loved one. Selecting a funeral home that projects a poor image through their advertising, diminishes the value of the tribute. Advertisements created by local cable stations, often with no appreciation for the intricacies of funeral service simply cannot project the quality image necessary to compete with other, quality-oriented funeral firms.

Buying media is a technical process just as any other business function. Professional media buyers assure you the best value, and often will reduce media budgets. This is particularly true in funeral service; few cable company employees appreciate the dynamics of funeral home selection; as such they are incapable of recommending an appropriate media schedule.

Just as with any advertising media, cable television requires time to work. The strength of cable television is the low cost for repetition. Commit to a one-year schedule of at least 30 weeks; it's the frequency and repetition that make it effective.

With cable's advantages of credibility, reach, frequency, audience targeting and low cost, it should be the primary medium utilized by funeral firms.

Your Web Site's Role in Effective Communication

Presently, only several thousand funeral homes nationally have a productive Web site. Many funeral home sites are unproductive either because the site's address is too unwieldy for consumers to remember or the consumer has no reason to revisit the site.

To remain actively competitive, a growth-oriented funeral home must include a productive Web site as an integral element of its advertising and promotional strategy. The Internet will not replace other media advertising but will supplement them. 60% of families with a funeral home preference base their preference on past experience.

As such, to build market share and volume, an aggressive funeral firm must cause consumers to rethink their priorities. The consumer needs information if they are to make a better decision. Traditionally this was accomplished through full-color brochures, public speaking and newspaper advertising; all of which are productive and necessary.

A productive Web site enables a funeral home to deliver timely information at a fraction of the cost of a printed brochure. The interactive elements of the site make it interesting, which causes repeat visits. The Internet allows you to effectively communicate with a number of groups important to your success in addition to the general consumers' population such as prospective employees, vendors, local media and government offices.

Most early Web sites for funeral homes were designed as simple information sites. Many of these sites included amateur photography of facility interiors, typical funeral home advertising copy and the firm's history. All of which is interesting to the firm's owners, but gives the consumer little or no reason to patronize the firm. A Web site should be so much more, to the extent it becomes the central, most comprehensive statement of who you are, what makes your firm unique and demonstrates how selecting your firm will result in a superior experience compared to other funeral homes in the market.

Consumers will not likely learn about you by stumbling across your site through a search engine, but will more likely come to the site directly after prompting from some other marketing medium (for example, direct mail, cable television, newspaper display advertisement or obituary). As such, your Web site is the middle component in a communication plan designed to build identity and volume.

Direct mail, newspaper and television advertisement is intended to surface need in the prospective client's mind. They acknowledge their need by contacting your firm through your Web site. As such, the Web site is the second step in the communication chain, inviting the client to learn more about you in a non-threatening environment. Emerging from this exploration is a comfort level and overt permission to "sell" to them. They have retained control (that's why the Internet is defined as "information delivery in a user defined environment").

Often an image piece, such as a full-color brochure, is used as a follow-up to the prospect's visit to your Web site as a means of further demonstrating how your firm is superior.

Web Site Components

Entry Point: This is the first thing a user will see. It might be a traditional "home page" with an introduction and/or clear links to other parts of the site, or it might be a "splash page" with an animated sequence that appears before the bulk of the site. If you use the latter, be sure the user can punch through the initial sequence without delay. Navigation should allow movement from any single place to any other single place in no more than two clicks.

A business Web site isn't a video game where visitors hunt around for an entry point. In general, don't plan your site for a one-time visitor, instead build elements into the site to foster repeat visits. For example, a listing of community events gives people a reason to visit the site monthly. The "Community Activities" listing should be easily resourced from the first page.

Although the site should be consumer oriented, it must be informational as opposed to entertaining. The focus should be content that is organized and presented well. This would exclude information that highlights the personal interests of employees, owners or superfluous information about the owner's family.

At-need Service Orientation: As many "First Call" staff members know, families typically have questions before meeting with a funeral director to make arrangements. Your Web site can include an Orientation Page that explains the first call process, the arrangement meeting, visitations, and the funeral. Cremation choices can be presented along with a list of local cemeteries and some of the cemetery rules and restrictions.

Legal: Identify any appropriate copyright and trademark/service market holders, and if the site offers any advice, include a disclaimer. This is particularly true in regard to aftercare, pre-need funding issues and prices.

Positioning Statement: State clearly how your funeral home differs from others in the market. Because most consumers believe all funeral homes to be the same, they have no reason not to return to the firm their family used previously. The objective of your funeral home Web site is to punctuate the differences in terms to which the consumer can readily relate.

Focus: If your competitive advantage is multiple facilities, the site should include a map of the area highlighting your many facilities. If your firm is one of a few or the only to have your own crematory, the site should include photos of your cremation facility. The same applies to issues of ownership (local versus corporate), aftercare services, pre-need, combinations, and other special features.

Prices Should Also Be Discussed: As many Internet-based retailers have learned through painful experience, the Web is a shopper's resource, but not necessarily a place to buy. Funeral home shoppers want to compare prices. As such, your Web site should demonstrate how your firm offers flexibility in services and prices centered upon serving their family with value-based pricing.

Contact Information: Nothing frustrates Web users more than having to hunt for contact information. List your phone number, street addresses, email addresses, maps and driving directions, as well as a form for additional information.

Employment Postings: The scarcity of licensed funeral directors nationally and the growing demand for death services demands that your firm exercise every opportunity to recruit. The most likely employment candidate, one inclined to relocate to another city or state, is relatively young and likely very comfortable using the Internet. Every funeral home Web site should include a page directed toward employment candidates.

Interaction Pages: The most utilized functions of a funeral home site are those that deliver information and facilitate interaction. The fundamental objective of all funeral home advertising is to answer consumers' questions. As a result, many funeral home sites include a "Frequently Asked Questions" function; but they include only a few questions and limited answers. A comprehensive FAQ would require hundreds of questions on every aspect of funeral services with expansive answers.

Very few consumers will pre-arrange and pre-pay funeral services online, but they will take time to complete a personal diary with personal information necessary for making pre-arrangements. As such, your sight should accommodate this interest while also collecting identifying information for follow-up by pre-need counselors.

Also, this information should be transmitted via secured lines to protect the privacy of the consumer and their family.

Presently, the most popular funeral home Web site function is Web-based obituaries. This service can be provided very inexpensively, and does not require a national service. Instead, posting obituaries on your own site can be as easy as cut and paste.

When visiting Web-based obituaries, many families will want to forward condolences, or even send flowers, sympathy cards or food baskets. All of these functions should be easily accessible and can be provided inexpensively, or at no cost at all other than hosting charges from a value-added host.

The possibilities for funeral service on the Internet are endless. To exploit the possibilities completely, it is important the site be integrated with your firm's total communication strategy. As such, the company you select to create your site may be the most important decision you make. Web site development companies often concentrate more on the technical aspect of the site than they do the communication and promotional functions.

Summary: As anyone who has ever talked to a teenager about the Internet knows, creating a simple Web site is a simple process. The challenge is to create a productive, cost-efficient Web site that can contribute to the accomplishment of your marketing objectives. This requires more than a programmer. In fact, Web site development is as much a challenge of graphic arts and copy writing, as it is programming. For this reason, many of the most productive Web sites come from marketing and advertising firms.

CHAPTER 8

Ten Reasons to Advertise

#1

Build brand loyalty. Funeral businesses traditionally have thrived from customer loyalty, which is another way of saying "brand loyalty." Over a period of time, a consumer develops expectations as to how a company will perform. An established "brand name" is a business' commitment to meet their client's expectations.

Nationally, many funeral homes define the "brand name" concept. Having been part of a community from 50 to 100 + years, residents of a community come to have definite ideas as to what they can expect from the various funeral firms in their community.

A consistent advertising theme (along with the firm's consistently high standards of service) creates loyalty for the firm so strong it can withstand the challenge from lower-priced competition, pre-need solicitations and other marketing efforts.

Loyalty to brand names is diminishing. The importance to a funeral business of building a strong brand name has not. It may take a greater effort to build a strong brand name, but the benefits will also be greater due to the decline of so many funeral homes.

#2

Competition for the funeral consumers' attention will be greater in the coming years than at any time in the past.

- The start-up of Internet casket stores,
- The increased effort by cemeteries to sell caskets and vaults,
- The shift in priority from acquisition to operations by the national corporations,
- The efforts by product manufacturers to advertise directly to the consumer,
- The growth of discount funeral service.

All of these factors will result in more death services advertising; the consumer will be awash in funeral service information. Maintaining business in this environment will demand a strong visibility.

#3

Mobility among all age groups is creating a large population without a local funeral home preference. Research studies conducted in the 1980's indicated 75% of consumers had a funeral home preference. Studies conducted in 2000 and 2001 indicate that number has fallen to approximately 55% in metro areas. Also, consumers' commitment to their preferred funeral home is not as strong as in the past. As such, advertising has a greater opportunity for success. In contrast, not advertising has greater risks than in the past.

#4

Flexibility in services and prices are the most important factors for consumers without a funeral home preference. Baby boomer adults selecting a funeral home for parents, often times from out of state, are much more influenced by information gleaned from advertising than people who have resided in the community a long period of time. Printed brochures and informative, easy to find Web sites are critical in today's competitive funeral industry.

#5

Increased emphasis on special services and facilities are important factors in a family's selection of a funeral home.

- Aftercare
- Personalization of funeral services
- Children's rooms and community lounges
- Memorial options with cremation
- Death away from home services

Because these features are relatively new in many communities, consumers may not be familiar with these innovations. Advertising these issues allows the consumer to take them into consideration when selecting a funeral home.

#6

Increased emphasis on pre-need. There is significant growth in the third-party selling business. Third-party sellers are making a definite impression on the pre-need productivity of their client funeral homes. Insurance companies are proactively promoting directly to consumers as opposed to depending upon the funeral home to carry the pre-need message. Both of these vendor groups represent competition to a funeral home attempting to market their own pre-need.

#7

Consumers' expectations are changing. One of the principle objectives of advertising is to demonstrate how a funeral home is in sync with the consumers' expectations. Funeral home advertising today addresses issues not raised in the past.

#8

Changes in ownership and staff have caused consumers to reconsider their funeral home preferences. First, many leading local funeral homes were acquired by national corporations, which resulted in significant staff changes. No sooner did the consumer get comfortable with the idea of a national funeral home chain, the funeral facility is sold to another individual. The second most often volunteered reason for preferring a funeral home is knowing a staff member. Changes in ownership demand advertising to introduce owners, managers and staff to the community.

#9

Periodically the FTC's, OSHA's, and other governmental agencies' activities relative to funeral service make the news. The government's interest in funeral services causes some people to assume some wrongdoing by members of the profession. Image advertising communicates a firm's values and principles. Just as other industries have, funeral homes must maintain a positive stream of information to counter the negative information coming from outside the industry.

#10

Consumers consult new and different sources for information and entertainment.

- Newspaper subscriptions have diminished 1% every six months for the past ten years. In contrast, approximately 70% of homes subscribe to cable television.
- Consumer mobility *(# 3 above)* results in fewer people reading the obituaries. Retirees moving to a new area don't know anyone in town, so they ignore the obituary page.
- Internet use by seniors compounds monthly.

For funeral home advertising to be successful, media selection must be in sync with consumers' lifestyles.

CHAPTER 9

How Advertising Works

Anyone who has devoted even a minimal amount of time to consider the challenge of selling (either through advertising, direct sales, or even from the larger perspective of marketing) knows that consumers use logic to rationalize their purchases, but the buying decision is made from their heart. There is an emotional basis to every buying decision. A popular airport bookstore marketing book, "Hot Button Marketing" by Barry Feig, codifies emotional decision making by identifying 16 emotional motivators; listed below.

1. The desire for control.
2. I'm better than you.
3. The excitement of discovery.
4. Revaluing.
5. Family values.
6. The desire to belong.
7. Fun is its own reward.
8. Poverty of time.
9. The desire to get the best.
10. Self achievement.
11. Sex, love, romance.
12. The nurturing response.
13. Reinventing oneself.
14. Make me smarter.

15. Power, dominance, influence.

16. Wish fulfillment.

Certainly, there could be a discussion as to whether there are truly 16 unique emotional motivators, and how much one overlaps with another, such as reinventing oneself versus revaluing. Nonetheless, identifying and naming the emotional motivators facilitates a conversation on selling and advertising. Mr. Feig's strategy to selling is to link the buyers "Hot Button" with your product.

Theoretically, if you identify the prospect's hot button (emotional motivator) and demonstrate how your product satisfies that emotional need, then the prospect will provide the logic necessary to rationalize the sale. For example, logically people by prepared soups for convenience and nutrition. But the unidentified emotional need is to satisfy one's need to nurture and to maintain family values.

An automobile is purchased for transportation, but the selection of a particular model can relate to sexuality, power, romance, being the best and having the best. Auto salespeople are authorities on hot button selling.

Now, review the above list to identify the motivators as they apply to death care services and products. Your first impression is that only a few apply to funeral services and memorialization. Nonetheless some do:

- The desire for control.
- I'm better than you.
- Family values.
- The desire to belong.
- The desire to get the best.
- The nurturing response.
- Wish fulfillment.

The question is this, "Does the typical family experiencing a death identify the above emotional needs and motivators with a funeral?" If you're honest with yourself, you'll have to answer no. Appreciating this point is critical in marketing death care services. The consumer does not understand how funeral home services help them which is why they challenge prices and comparison shop.

If a 40 year old, recently divorced male walks into a Porsche dealership, even the dimmest salesperson will immediately realize that the prospect is not there for transportation. Instead, he is interested in acquiring the means for facilitating new relationships.

A shoe salesperson helping a middle-aged woman in the selection of uncomfortable designer shoes for $500 plus, knows that what she is really purchasing is a weapon in the perceived battle she wages daily with younger women.

The realtor selling a home in an upscale neighborhood knows her prospect is seeking upward mobility.

What is our prospect seeking? When a family walks into a funeral home and says we don't want any services, just minimal cremation. That is evidence that they have not made a link between the death care purchase and their emotional needs or motivators. Certainly, the funeral satisfies some needs, but families are not seeing it. How do we, as an industry, help them make the link?

The answer is advertising. Your advertising objective is to help the consuming public in your community to make the connection between your services and their emotional motivators. Productive advertising demonstrates the emotional payback a family receives. You have probably read articles about advertising where the author related to the need for an emotional payback in advertising. Productive funeral home advertising uses emotional messages to demonstrate the need for funerals, memorials and personalization.

Within the industry there is a great deal of grousing and complaining about the consumer's lack of loyalty, and confusion as to why there are so many price shoppers, and why minimal cremation is rampant, and why don't children love their parents? The solution to the challenges in death care cannot be found by blaming consumers. Consumers do not perceive themselves as losing or sacrificing anything of value when they opt for minimal disposal. The challenge in demonstrating this is ours, not theirs.

Some industries and professions have sufficiently affluent national associations that support their local efforts with national advertising campaigns, such as the dairy producers popular "Got Milk" campaign. Death care associations do not have the financial resources to launch a national campaign. However, the funeral profession actually has a track record of advertising success. The fact that billions of dollars are held in trust accounts and insurance policies is evidence of the impact of the combined productivity of thousands of independent businesses promoting a single concept. As funeral homes and cemeteries nationally advertised their own individual pre-need services, the consumer heard a single message. Pre-need satisfies real needs:

- Peace of mind of knowing the decisions are made
- Freeing family from making decisions at a difficult time
- Controlling costs
- Expressing one's own thoughts and priorities, even after they are deceased

As a result of this singular, prolonged message, 50% of consumers age 45+ intend to make funeral prearrangements at some point, and approximately 30% of consumers age 65+ already have. What effect could a singular, prolonged message regarding the value of the funeral and memorialization have on consumers' at-need decisions?

But when it comes to fundamental advertising (advertising that explains the benefits of our primary products), there is nearly a complete void. If one examines cemetery advertising, which has focused on free veteran spaces since WWII, (apparently emotion is absent in the purchase of cemetery products), instead the prospect is only interested in the number of free burial spaces they can secure.

Why does cemetery advertising not discuss the need for memorialization, particularly as it applies to cremation. Fewer than 5% of consumers relate to the term "columbarium." Few consumers know cemeteries offer scattering gardens and ossuaries. Is there any surprise that the majority of consumers preferring cremation intend to personally scatter the cremated remains? Is it any wonder that potentially millions of temporary urns are stored in closets nationally? The consumer does not have the information they need to make intelligent decisions, and it is the industries' challenge to educate them. But instead of information, our advertising focuses on "Buy one, get one free."

In recent years, many funeral homes nationally have adopted "Drive Safely" advertising campaigns. What does this say about your funeral home's offerings and how they satisfy emotional needs? The only conclusion the consumer can make is that death care services offer nothing of value. They charge $6000 to $10,000 dollars for a three-day service for which there is no redeemable value. But we, within the industry, know there is. We simply don't tell anyone, assuming that the public will figure it out on their own. Well, they're not.

Local Competition:

One of the most interesting facets of the competition between funeral businesses on a local basis is the frustration large volume firms suffer in their on-going competition with far smaller competitors. A large volume firm, with multiple facilities, typically does not compete with similar sized companies. Instead, they will compete with far smaller businesses, typically a single facility, serving anywhere from 50 to 200 families annually. The larger firm offers convenience, on-site crematories, reception rooms, counselors, often they offer the convenience of a funeral home on or near their own cemetery. With all of these advantages and benefits, how do little, stand-alone businesses compete?

Research studies conducted by MKJ indicate that single facilities offer benefits large companies cannot. A family calling a 100-call firm will likely speak directly to the owner. The first call team will likely include the owner, a relative, or a long term, trusted employee. The embalming will likely be accomplished or at least supervised by the owner. Arrangements will be made with the owner, and his wife will serve refreshments. When the family arrives for visitation, they are greeted by the owner, and escorted throughout the facility. This is a level of personal service large funeral businesses cannot match, and families know that.

Another consumer assumption, which the large corporations have reinforced over the past decade, is that larger volume firms have higher prices than single facility operations.

So, if the small volume funeral firm has inherent advantages in their competition with the large firms, what competitive advantages should the larger firm possess?

- Facility features as listed above
- Larger promotional budgets.
- Better trained staff members
- Convenience
- Better value by offering more diverse options

How are these advantages effectively communicated through a "Drive Safely" advertising campaign? They're not.

What message does the consumer receive from "Drive Safely?" Maybe they assume you care about their general well being; but do you really think your neighbors are so cynical as to believe that you, as a death care professional, hope that they will be killed driving their cars? No. What they derive from these advertisements is that their basic assumption is correct, funeral homes offer nothing of value, and there is very little difference between one funeral business and another, so you might as well use the closest, cheapest place you can find. Which, of course, explains the success of minimal cremation providers over the past 15 years.

Summary: Most funeral business owners know they should invest somewhere in the range of 3.5% of gross sales (at-need and pre-need) in advertising annually. Most marketing leaders invest two to three times that much. But what is the message they are sending the public?

Many of the under-40 children who are now coming in to ownership of well-established funeral homes will introduce themselves as "different from my dad and grandfather." Many will go so far as to say, "I'm not like most funeral directors." The reality is, from a marketing and business management perspective, today's new owners are shockingly and painfully similar to their fathers and grandfathers. They may dress differently, and they don't attend conventions as often, but their decision making has not changed. They are not training their arrangers, and today's advertising efforts are as void of effective messages as they ever were.

Making a funeral business profitable, demands that management makes the right moves; and, for the most part, we are not doing that yet

CHAPTER 10

Building a Brand People Can Hate

Think about a product you truly love; it doesn't matter what the product is; but it has to be a brand to which you are completely committed. Consumers develop a commitment to a product when it meets their needs and expectations so perfectly, that even when they try a competitive product, it only serves to strengthen their loyalty. There are products like this; clothes, golf clubs, automobiles, churches, food products, sports teams, restaurants, the list goes on and on, including funeral homes. What is it about a product that creates absolute customer commitment?

Consumers love products that meet their needs exactly. Consumer passion occurs when the producer of that product or service understands the consumer that product was created for, and have successfully reached them with their message. Just as sure as they have found their customer, they have also alienated other consumers. Just as one demographic of consumers loves the product, another body of consumers is equally certain the product is not for them. They may even resent anyone who uses that product.

When developing a successful brand strategy, it is critical to identify the consumer for which the brand is being developed because it's the emotion the consumer of the product develops that is the foundation of their loyalty. Any product or brand that creates customer passion is, by definition, not for everyone.

Funeral home owners, like all business people, want to serve everyone, and they want everyone to buy their best product. There's nothing unusual about that; every business wants the same thing, but in a world where consumers have a broad spectrum of options and every consumer is demanding, it not realistic to capture 100% of the market. Attempting to be everything to everybody will simply result in a product lacking identity, and with no customer loyalty.

But it is realistic to capture all or most of the business from those prospects that your product was created for. Some products and services can survive without an identity; death care businesses (cemeteries, funeral homes, cremation services) are more successful when consumers have a good understanding and appreciation of what the business stands for.

Most communities have a funeral home that is clearly seen as the quality leader. Typically this firm will have the highest prices and the largest volume. The owners of other funeral homes in the community try to understand what makes the leader so successful, why are people willing to pay more to use that firm versus theirs? They study the suits the funeral directors where, they copy the advertising, if the leader has a holiday grief seminar, several others in town will try the same. If the leader builds a crematory, so do the others. In simple terms, they compete by complimenting the leader; funeral businesses have been doing it forever with no success.

A strategy of complimenting the leader will never be successful; consumers willing to pay more to use the quality leader have good reasons for preferring that firm. Why would they shift their patronage to a funeral home that is trying to be just as good? When competing with the leader, there is only one proven strategy: contrast, not compliment.

Regardless of product or service, any time there has been a successful challenger to an industry leader it has been a strategy of contrast; being diametrically opposite the leader in a clear and discernible way.

- Pepsi convinced consumers that their product had a better taste, but the strategy was not successful in winning market share. What has been successful is positioning their product as being preferred by young people, and that Coke is their parents (and grandparents) drink.

- Many airlines have competed on the basis of being a better United, Delta or American Airlines; all of them have failed. Southwest Airlines is successful because they have positioned themselves as completely different. Instead of traditional airline suits, they wear Dockers and golf shirts. Instead of formal professionalism, the crew tells jokes, even when doing the safety presentations.

- Most chicken in grocery stores is priced as a commodity. Tyson sells chicken based upon the owner's persona, product quality that is supported by their higher price strategy.

- Apple successfully competes with the far larger IBM platform computers by capturing the graphic arts segment of the market and expanding their base from there.

- The entire auto industry is based upon niche marketing; every single vehicle and each brand name is designed to differentiate itself in some way from every other vehicle.
- The apparel industry is a complex myriad of competing brand names. Within each major category are brands attempting to appeal to a specific demographic group.

The first step in implementing a segmentation strategy is to identify the characteristics of the targeted group. Who do we want to serve and what is important to them; not in terms of funeral service, but in terms of their self esteem? All funeral homes conduct funerals, talking about funerals will not differentiate one funeral home from another. In some situations, facilities, personalization, cremation services, pre-need or other special services can differentiate one firm from another, but in many communities even these issues are too similar among competitors. There are times when the only real difference between competing funeral homes is their promotional message. Is your advertising reaching someone or are you just buying time or space?

Seniors look for surrogate families to replace the family they have lost over time. Many funeral directors relate stories of how seniors will telephone the funeral home to advise them that they have not had as many listings in the obituaries as have some of the other firms in town, and to offer advice on how to market their services. These people obviously identify with that funeral firm at a level far above simply being a local business. They have attended funerals there, have come to know the staff, and have a sense of identification with the firm. The highest levels of Maslow's hierarchy of needs, self-actualization, is often referred to when analyzing why people do what they do. Self-actualization is a very intriguing motivation, for some people it is a driving force in their life. But further down the spectrum, impacting a far larger number of people, is the need for belonging; only two needs (sustenance and security) are more vital to human survival than is belonging. For many funeral homes, giving seniors a sense of identification with their firm is their primary challenge. The second most common reason volunteered for preferring a funeral home is knowing someone on the staff. When staff members build a local identity with seniors, they are facilitating a sense of "belonging" with the funeral home.

Funeral homes have the greatest difficulty connecting with the affluent and well-educated consumer. Affluent consumers are simply uninterested in what funeral homes have to offer. Changing this is a matter of effectively communicating with wealthy consumers. Accomplishing that is a matter of understanding what's important to them.

- Foremost, affluent people want other people to know they are successful. What other possible reason can be given to explain the buying decisions they make?
- Second, they want to be treated special. Meeting with an unprepared, unimpressive arranger will not encourage them to spend more. On the other hand, meeting with one of the owners of the firm, who is well versed and knowledgeable in cremation options and services can convert this family from minimal services to personalized memorials and higher quality merchandise.
- Often, the affluent consumer takes the form of a baby boomer representing their parents. If the key in brand development is to create an image that consumers can identify with; or better put, letting the customer "own" the brand, what can we do to let the baby boomer "own" your brand? We'd begin by building the brand around what we know about baby boomers:
    - Baby boomers respond very well to packaging, not just packages of services and products, but actual packaging. They respond to the way the product is presented. Notice how restaurant menus have evolved from being simply informative, to being graphic and artistic. Check into even a mid-priced hotel, they give you a key packaged in a portfolio with hotel information. Buy a new car and the documentation comes in a leather portfolio. Baby boomers love packaging.

      Look at how your firm presents cremation choices; do you use an arrangement presentation, or do you expect your arranger to verbally describe all of the options available with cremation? Just having a presentation tool will greatly influence the final sale.

- Baby boomers watch television. More than any other identifying characteristic, baby boomers are addicted to television for entertainment and information just as the WWII generation were avid newspaper readers, and the depression era listened to the radio and younger generations identify with the computer.

  Baby boomers do not read the newspaper, and certainly not the obituary page.

- Baby boomers reject anything valued by their parents. Their parents want to do "what is right," and "the same thing everyone else does." Baby boomers want to do what is right for them, and above all, they don't want what everyone else does.

- Baby boomers reject aging, and identify with new. Although many baby boomers love old architecture, they want it updated and fresh. A funeral home in an old building can capture baby boomers, but not with old furnishings, in small, dimly lit rooms. Do away with the drapes, open the windows, and polish the hardwood floors.

- Baby boomers are the sandwich generation caught between the expense of educating their children and caring for their parents. They are cash strapped, shop for discounts, and only spend money when they derive benefits of value to them. Simply giving them a deal on a better quality casket, an extra night of visitation, or a newer hearse won't build brand loyalty.

Walmart television advertisements communicate effectively with baby boomer women by showing prices physically dropping on their television advertisements. Contrary to nearly every other form of price advertising, the Walmart advertisements don't specify on what products the customer will save money. The objective of their advertisements is to build an image of offering lower prices, in general. What image does your funeral home communicate to baby boomers? Do you tell them your firm is affordable, is responsive to their wishes, offers services they want, or is the right choice for their parents?

Summary: No one will ever predict that the "best days" in death care are ahead of us. They are definitely behind us, and will never return in the same form as in the past. As a result, not every funeral home, and certainly not every cemetery, will survive the coming shake out. Instead, the best marketed firms, those that understand their market and successfully sell into it, will do well even as others disappear. If you don't have a clear picture of your challenges, opportunities and goals, you may want to work late tonight getting it together.

CHAPTER 11

What Makes a Funeral Home a Leading Firm?

Across the U.S. and Canada, there are many very good quality funeral firms. But there are probably only about 500 "leading" funeral homes.

MKJ Marketing conducts research studies nationally. In most communities all of the competing funeral homes have similar name awareness, and consumers' perception of one firm is very similar to that of the others. But in some markets there is a funeral home that dominates the consumer's awareness. These firms are truly different from the others. Given time, leading funeral homes tend to be volume leaders and more financially successful.

What Are the Common Attributes of "Leading" Funeral Homes?

Facilities: Historically, funeral service focused more on facilities and personal service than other elements of the business. Because convenience is an important element of quality funeral service, leading firms were, and continue to be, the first to branch.

Leading funeral homes take particular pride in the décor of their funeral homes. Their facilities are typified by bright colors, flooding natural light, contemporary, fresh appearing furniture and well planned floor plans. These characteristics are present, even in remodeled facilities.

Because of the special attention devoted to their facilities resulting in a continuum of building or remodeling projects, they are the first to implement innovations in facilities.

Public reception rooms, smoking rooms, clergy rooms and, most recently, children's rooms are common at leading funeral homes.

Contrary to average funeral homes, the leading funeral firms appreciate the priorities of those families that prefer cremation disposition. That is why they were the first to build their own crematories. Often located on site, the crematory allows the leading funeral firm to provide a special convenience and service other firms cannot. As opposed to transporting the deceased across county or state lines, transferring them to other companies, leading firms maintain quality control by employing their own staff and equipment.

These same firms are the first to build *cremation tribute centers* which provide specially designed facilities to better serve the cremation-oriented family.

Special Services: Leading firms maintain a close vigilance on the changing priorities of the consumer. As a result they are the first to incorporate new, value-added services. Over the past twenty years, new services included pre-need, aftercare, and cremation services. Presently these same firms are the first to train staff and the public as to how personalization adds meaning to a funeral with little or no additional cost.

Quality of Staff: ""A" people hire "A" people. "B" people hire "C" people." Donald Rumsfeld. A quality organization is comprised of quality people. They are visibly superior to others, and demonstrate their superior capabilities in their appearance and their ability to interact with the public both verbally and in writing.

The leading firms build quality people through consistent training and motivational efforts. They hold their quality people through better than average compensation and benefits.

Because "A" people endeavor to excel daily, they need to know what is expected of them. This is why leading funeral firms are committed to established policies and procedures. Larger firms are now employing Human Resource Managers to allow them to maintain a professional work environment for their growing staffs.

Reputation: Over 400 market research studies conducted nationally and in Canada over the past twenty years demonstrate that leading funeral homes build and sustain an impeccable reputation. Because management and staff are well aware of the organization's position, the market and priorities, they are able to establish standards and maintain them over a long period of time.

Because the public expects to pay a little more for quality, and because they perceive so much value from a quality firm, market leaders combine what many would consider counterintuitive; high volume and higher prices.

Because leading funeral homes have grown in volume, they are not typically perceived as being affiliated with one religious or ethnic group more than another. They appreciate the ceremonial needs of each segment of their community and incorporate these requirements into their facilities.

Established Lines of Communication: Leading funeral homes appreciate the need to communicate to their customers and to those families that have not yet experienced their superior standards. As such, all leading funeral homes employ diverse communication efforts, including informative brochures on cremation, pre-need, personalization, funeral etiquette, grief and special needs, such as death away from home. Leading firms are the first to adapt to new technology, such as cable television and Web sites while also expanding the capabilities of billboard, newspaper, direct mail and newspaper inserts.

Market research analysts, when conducting consumer research concerning consumer products and professional services, have observed that research respondents typically will name their favored brand (the one they would actually use themselves) first when asked to name all of the brands they can think of.)

Contrary to this situation, in funeral service research respondents will often name a leading funeral home first, even when they intend to patronize another funeral home. This is one of the most visible ways in which consumer behavior differs toward funeral homes compared to other products and services. Because consumers have patronized a funeral home in the past, they are inclined to return to that firm even if they know it is not their best option.

This illustrates how leading firms grow their volume over a matter of decades. They may not be able to pull a family away from a competitor immediately, but by being consistently superior, they will ultimately get a chance to serve a family. Once they have broken into that family, leading firms seldom lose them.

Because leading firms will develop a clearly discernible image in their advertising, the public recognizes the logos of leading funeral firms simply from the repetitive exposure.

Leading firms take every opportunity to participate and be visible in their community through public relations efforts. Leading firms sponsor holiday grief programs, public education programs, as well as professional in-service training programs for hospice and nursing professionals, clergy, law enforcement and other caring professionals.

In many communities, certain individuals will surface as the recognized authority in a specific profession or area of interest. It is not unusual for a banker to be more visible than other people employed in the banking industry locally. This individual will be interviewed by the press on matters relating to banking, or consulted by other local leaders.

In funeral service marketing, there is no position more important to the success of a funeral home than being the recognized "death expert." Becoming the recognized death authority demands effort; writing articles, public speaking, being available to assist groups even when there is little or no chance the firm will realize any immediate business from the effort. Leading funeral homes recognize the value of being the "death expert" and are willing to devote the time and effort necessary to capture the title.

Because leading funeral homes are sensitive to the consumers' changing demands and expectations, they are the first to explore the possibilities of alternative service levels or business concepts. Just like they were the first to offer pre-need, even when others attempted to defeat the concept through legislation; and just as they were the first to promote the availability of cremation services.

Many of these leaders were the first to combine the services of a funeral home on a cemetery. The success of early cemetery/mortuary combinations caused the national consolidation companies to attempt to mass produce combinations thinking it was the combination concept that was a success versus the much more subtle influence of superior management and marketing.

Today the leaders of these firms are learning how to profitably operate lower cost funeral service alternatives with offsite arrangement centers, chapel services, and/or discount funeral homes. Again, others will observe the success of the low cost alternatives and will attempt to transfer it only to meet with frustration. The key to successfully operating a low cost alternative is not the low cost; instead it is the more subtle influence of superior management and marketing.

Marketing: Too many small business owners and managers, marketing is just another word for advertising; and advertising is another word for contributions in the form of church bulletin ads and calendars. Marketing is the totality of the business, including position in the market, consumer niches, location, price, image, staff and facilities.

Managers at leading funeral businesses established a perspective of their firm's long-term direction. They know why and when to buy, build or remodel facilities long in advance because of their comprehension of the market and dynamics that determine success and failure. It is for this reason they have more successes than failures when expanding.

Management: Whether due to necessity or intent, leading funeral homes implement outstanding systems of management and supervision. As these firms have grown, one area of constant concern has been what is said and done by funeral directors in arrangement meetings. Management has specific expectations relative to the information provided families during the arrangement session. In order to make good decisions, families need all of the pertinent information. Whether the arranging funeral director relays this information to the family, and how it is communicated is of critical importance to larger firms that may have as many as 30 to 50 arrangers.

Many firms accomplish this through arrangement kits. The arrangement kits are an example of the management systems leading firms implement to assure a consistent standard of service.

In addition to operational systems, management at leading funeral homes has learned to delegate. A single individual cannot effectively manage larger operations. They can be dominated, which simply means the organization learns not to function unless specifically directed by the owner. Many businesses fail to grow simply because key managers were incapable of delegating authority.

The most difficult challenge for many funeral home owners is to answer the question "Why would a family not choose our firm?" Regardless of the scale of their firm's liabilities, some owners and managers are simply incapable of comprehending why the public would choose another funeral home.

Good managers are capable of stepping outside the organization to examine their business objectively. It is through this process they are able to conceive opportunities for improvement as well as opportunities for growth. In contrast, second tier business managers visualize from within the confines of their present business. They never change simply because they cannot visualize circumstances different from how they are.

Summary: What makes leading firms special is not that they are large volume firms. What makes them leaders are that the elements of their operations make them different. Over time, the differences between the leading firms and other funeral homes results in greater financial success; this allows them to charge more for their services, insulates them from discounters while allowing them to build new facilities and to expand their service areas. Ultimately, leading funeral homes become volume leaders.

Thus any firm can become a leading funeral home given time and a commitment to excellence. One funeral home operation run excellently will enable the firm to grow in volume and financial success.

CHAPTER 12

How Followers Become Leaders

In most markets, there are three funeral home positions:

- Leaders
- Followers
- Lower priced

Although there are a growing number of exceptions, typically the lower-priced firm does poorly, in that they attempt to provide all of the services the leaders and followers do, but at a lower price. Simply put, many firms with lower prices fail to grasp the simple fact that a low-price strategy only succeeds with volume, and the volume won't come without aggressive advertising.

The leading funeral homes are those with the higher-priced, finer facilities, and will typically set the standard for services in their communities.

The most interesting firms to study are the followers; they are typically less creative than the leaders, and in some ways more pathetic than the lower-priced firms. At least the lower priced firms have a concept as to how they can differentiate themselves from the others. Followers are inclined to watch the leader, and attempt to duplicate or match their innovations, but typically will not commit fully to the effort. As such, they flounder year after year, trying to understand why the leaders continue to prosper, and how they're better than the lower priced firms.

The tragedy in the plight of the "follower" is that what is needed to enhance their competitive position is usually quite simple, and affordable. In fact, over the long term, their business would be more profitable as their volume grows. Followers advertise, but unlike the leaders, they invest their advertising dollars without the benefit of intelligent thought; every year they set aside a budget to be expended on the same efforts they invested in the year before, and the year before that. The fact that their investment would certainly seemed to have failed only serves to convince them that advertising doesn't work.

The first objective when setting an advertising budget is to identify what it is you're trying to accomplish. For most funeral homes, the target audience for their advertising are consumers between ages 55-64; they have lived within ten miles of the funeral home for at least fifteen years, and they are solidly middle income, or higher. (There is very little financial gain in serving low-income families. Most of them simply have little or no money and truly can not afford the services most funeral homes want to provide, with the exception of ethnic populations who will spend disproportionate to their income for funeral services.)

Given that the above demographics represents the target audience for funeral home advertising, most funeral home owners would be hard pressed to present a logical explanation as to why they invest their meager advertising budget as they do. For the most part, funeral homes invest in three forms of advertising:

- Yellow pages
- Newspaper display ads
- Pre-need letters provided by insurance companies

Given the fact that most consumers selecting a funeral home have resided in the community for at least fifteen years, and are somewhat older, these people are well aware of their funeral home options. By definition, an individual selecting a funeral home from the yellow pages would have to be unchurched, few friends, and no relatives in the area. Nonetheless, many funeral homes will invest as much as 50% of their advertising budget hoping to snag the 5% or few families that research indicate would refer to the yellow pages when selecting a funeral home; in reality fewer than 1% actually do.

90% of the newspaper advertisements run by funeral homes appear on the obituary page, even though very few residents ages 55-64 ever glance at the obits. Newspaper subscriptions have declined 1% every six months for the past twenty years simply because baby boomers don't read the newspaper, choosing to get their news from cable television and the Internet. Just like yellow page advertising, the newspaper advertising budget will routinely fail to produce results.

Certainly, pre-need is an important part of funeral home marketing, and every funeral home should have at least one person dedicated to pre-need sales. But investing in printing and postage for pre-need survey letters time and time again is a dysfunctional mode of lead generation, let alone advertising.

For funeral home advertising to be successful, the reader must have some reason to shift their patronage away from one funeral home in deference to another. Fundamentally, when the family meets at 2:00 AM in the foyer of the nursing home, hospice or hospital, unless someone in the family has a good reason not to, they are going to call the funeral home they have used in the past. The objective of your advertising is to give them a good reason to call you.

Research studies conducted by MKJ Marketing indicate the most significant special services or features a funeral home could offer are:

- Own and operate your own crematory
- Offer personalized and individualized services
- Offer the convenience of a reception or community room where the family can meet following services
- Offer competitive prices

But even more important than special services and facility features that all leading funeral homes share, and typically represents their greatest asset, is a strong brand name. A brand name represents a promise to the consumer; a commitment to provide a certain level of service, within a certain price range. When consumers buy a Sony electronics product, they are willing to pay a premium to get the Sony commitment. Lesser products lack the brand name, and cannot charge as much.

There is no business where the value of the brand name is more apparent than death care. The premium cemetery charges more than all the others, has less difficulty generating leads, getting appointments, or making sales. Leading funeral homes are impacted less by lower priced competitors, charge more, and grow faster than other funeral businesses. During the consolidation period of the 1990's, the acquiring firms were anxious to overpay for funeral homes with strong brand names, with exceptionally high multiples for firms with multiple facilities sharing the same name.

Today, most of the acquisitions are being accomplished by family-owned businesses as they consolidate within their communities. Unfortunately, many of them failed to learn from the previous acquisition frenzy, and maintained the existing name, as opposed to introducing themselves to their new community. Certainly, maintaining the old name seems less risky up front; but there is very little evidence that it is an effective long-term strategy. Sooner instead of later, the community learns of the change in ownership, and many families will shift their patronage to another local firm where they know the staff and ownership. In reality, a safer strategy is to make every effort up front to sell families on the advantages offered by the new owners, even if it means reducing prices for a time until families come to appreciate the firm for the benefits it offers.

How to Build a Strong Brand

To have a brand image, the company must stand for something, and the consumer must know what that something is. The business communicates that something through memorable advertising. Eveready Battery did it with the mechanical drumming bunny. AFLAC did it with the quacking duck, and Chick-Fil-A did it with the cow billboards. Wendy's used Frank Thomas, Miller Lite did it with retired athletes quarreling over less filling/better taste. Donald Trump built his image on excess, Yellow Cab company did it with yellow cabs; Greyhound buses did it with "Leave the driving to us," Hertz put you in the driver's seat, and Avis tried harder as #2. AOL did it with an endless stream of start-up cd's. Wilbert Vault company built its image with decades of service, BCC planted trees in national forests and twenty years of advertising in the Reader's Digest.

The point being, brand names are built, day-by-day, over a long period of time. The end result is a better operating company, generating superior profits, even during down times.

Funeral homes with strong brand names typically share certain attributes. They are aggressive in management, they take risks, and, most importantly, they commit to advertising and promotion. Because promotion also includes public relations efforts, leading firms are involved in that also

CHAPTER 13

Capturing the Position as the Alternative to the Leader

The challenge most funeral homes have is that another funeral home in their market has a firm grasp on the most desirable position. How should a funeral business position itself when the most desirable position is unattainable? For many funeral homes, the strategy is to position themselves as quality, but in contrast from the market leader.

For example, many consumers believe the market leader only does one kind of funeral. They have attended so many funerals at the leader's funeral home over many years, and for the most part, they all appeared to be about the same. As such, over time, people begin to think the leading firm does only one kind of funeral and it's expensive. Research studies conducted by MKJ Marketing for funeral home clients nationally include questions regarding the availability of cremation services from funeral homes in their community.

As much as 59% of consumers will indicate that a leading funeral home in their community does not provide cremation services, or that they do not know if that firm provides cremation services.

Contrasting a funeral home against the leader is a matter of understanding how consumers perceive the various firms in a market, and creating an advertising plan that takes advantage of the consumer's perceptions. This can be accomplished with personalization, flexibility, serving selected religious groups, and ownership.

For example, a client recently mentioned how no national corporation would offer an aftercare program similar to theirs because of the expense involved. This firm purchased a lovely, small home and invested in extensive remodeling to create a suitable facility for an aftercare center. The firm schedules grief-counseling groups throughout the week, and their investment in aftercare is significant, but what is the payback?

In this community of two funeral homes, what better way is there to demonstrate the difference between the national corporation and a family-owned firm, than by providing a special service the competitor can never match? Over time, the difference in the firms will become evident, even to the competitor's most-loyal clientele.

There are many special features and benefits available from family-owned funeral homes, national corporations simply will not, or cannot, match. Feature these differences in your advertising to reinforce the value perspective. While you can probably think of others, here are a few examples:

- The importance of selecting a funeral home that operates its own crematory
- Special talents and training of individual staff members
- Participation in civic events
- The advantages of a funeral home and cemetery operated by one company
- Holiday grief programs
- The convenience of multiple facilities
- Pet cemetery or crematory
- Local ownership of mausoleums

The objective of advertising is to verbalize your funeral home's assets in consumer terms. For example, most consumers would not immediately appreciate why it is important for a funeral home to operate their own crematory. Although some people are aware of the abuses committed by some commercial crematories, most consumers are not. For consumers to appreciate the difference, your advertising must effectively communicate the funeral home's high standard of service and professionalism.

Over time, through effective communication, families preferring cremation will willingly pay a premium for the perceived value of having the cremation performed locally by concerned professionals, as opposed to transferring the deceased to another company, often located in another city or county.

The Challenge of Discounting

It is impossible for many funeral facilities to attain the position of quality leader. Reputation, location, or the physical structure can preclude the consumer from ever perceiving some funeral homes as a quality leader. Nonetheless, these facilities can still be profitable; the second most desirable position is the low price leader. Low cost leaders can be very profitable, but again the strategy demands much more than just lower prices.

A significant number of discount retail concepts have failed during the 1980's and 90's. A recent article in the Wall Street Journal chronicled the rise and fall of category killers – retail stores that make it impossible for other retailers to compete in entire categories of consumer goods through high volume and low prices. For example, Home Depot has captured the market for Hunter ceiling fans, Weber Grills, quality brand hand tools and other products. Conceptually, the casket retail store would be considered a "category killer" because their objective is to undercut traditional casket prices so much as to preclude funeral home casket sales. (Just for the record, this isn't going to happen.)

As history will attest, discounting is a very tough business. It is particularly difficult for a funeral home, with an established clientele, to begin offering discount pricing and still realize a profit. Do the math:

A 100-call funeral home with an average sale of $4300 gross:	$430,000
A $1,000 discount reduces gross revenue by:	$100,000
Net sales after discount:	$330,000

To regain the lost revenue, this firm must serve an additional thirty cases at the discounted price just to break even. Increasing volume also increases overhead, however, and unless the volume increases significantly, the firm could very well conduct more funerals and generate less revenue, thereby reducing their profits.

Many funeral homes fail in the low price position simply because their cost of doing business is much greater than their prices. As such, the first challenge in capturing the low price position is to determine how the firm will profitably operate with lower prices. It isn't easy and demands the owner/operator to make hard decisions and to maintain strict discipline.

Ironically, operating successfully as a low price leader demands even more advertising than does the quality leader. The challenge is even greater in funeral service than in other industries because a funeral is a tribute. The target audience for discounted funeral services is people who really want a quality funeral, but can't afford the quality leader. As such, those families most likely to have a traditional funeral are unlikely to patronize a funeral home that has aggressively advertised low price. That is why most discount funeral concepts have a product mix of 80% minimal cremation. For the tribute to be meaningful, it must be dignified. The wrong kind of advertising can position the lower-priced funeral home as cheap and crass.

Competing with Discounters

The best, and only, defense against a price discounter, is to establish the value perspective in the consumers' mind. The American consumer is well educated and sensitive to value, so the challenge is to educate consumers to your firm's advantages.

When one company advertises service and value while another advertises lower prices, the consumer "positions" the two in their mind. They conclude that "one firm is good, the other is cheap." Admittedly, some people will consider price as the only priority and will select the low-cost firm. Often, in funeral service, this group represents the "no pays and slow pays." Families of means, special needs, a discerning sense of value, or sensitivity to the purpose of a funeral will select the "service oriented" firm. Over time, the value-based firm will build a clientele of quality business.

Staff Training

A funeral home staff member participating in an in-house training program once asked the trainer: " At what point do we refer a family to the lower-priced funeral home? I mean, at what price do we not want their business?" The speaker was stunned, as was the funeral owner, whose firm offered price packages competitive with any firm in its market and, like most funeral homes, contributed its services to the truly needy. From the associate's perspective, however, there had to be a price-point at which the firm would not want the business.

The question is, "Who is at fault for this type of thinking?" The staff associate or the owner? Obviously, in this case the associate had not received adequate training to accomplish their job. Success in a service business, regardless of the nature of the competition, demands a well-managed organization, and training is an important management function.

When staff is untrained, they are left to their own devices. When asked a question, associates will respond with an answer that seems reasonable to them at the time. It is management's responsibility to provide the answer which best reflects the company's policy.

Increase Your Visibility

Based upon research studies conducted throughout the United States and Canada, approximately 25 percent of consumers aged 35 and older expect a funeral to cost in excess of $7,500. Another 22 percent have no idea at all about the cost of a funeral. Ignorance of funeral costs and fees encourages consumers to consider purchasing the lower-price alternatives, they see advertised.

People today want to be informed, more so than in the past. That is why they respond to pre-need promotions, shop prices, and attend informative public seminars and other outreach efforts.

Facilitating communication between customers and businesses has been one of the driving forces of technological advancement throughout American industry for the past two decades resulting in the development of the Internet, cable advertising, infomercials, and toll-free telephone numbers, in addition to the traditional advertising media of broadcast television, radio, direct mail and billboards.

Because funeral homes are considered, "somber," the public is more reluctant to contact a funeral home than other types of businesses. Consequently, funeral homes should invest even more aggressively in their promotion than other types of businesses.

CHAPTER 14

Thinking Differently about Funeral Packages

Many funeral homes offer funeral packages. For the most part, they represent a better value than à la carte arrangements and help increase the average sale. But they can also be a problem when price shoppers are comparing funeral home prices. They think they want the lowest price, when what most of them really want is the best value.

The problem is that most funeral homes only offer one package when what we really need is multiple packages; good-better-best. The key in creating your set of packages is to build the package around what people want instead of what you want them to want.

Affluent consumers are accustomed to getting more because they are willing and able to pay more. An affluent consumer is more likely to buy one quality watch for $1500 or more that will last twenty years or more, than to buy a new watch every two years. The higher-priced watch, over the long term is a better value. Affluent customers can afford the better value of the higher-priced package.

The key to successful pricing is including elements in the packages they actually want. If this consumer is choosing between a package versus minimal or no services, an additional night of visitation does not represent a better value. What does?

- Valet parking
- Personalization
- Services conducted in the premium time slot
- The firm's best arranger
- The use of superior vehicles
- Internet services or functions

- Photographs of flowers identifying the giver
- Use of the superior chapel
- Use of the reception room
- Use of the children's room
- Having a family member or other representative present at the crematorium
- Reception catered with flatware and china; or
- Fresh baked cookies, coffee, and tea served after the service
- Concierge services

The above services represent services and functions some people would want. Others wouldn't want to pay for them; but some would. These elements should be included in the preferred package.

If all of the above are included in the only package offered, the service charge will be much higher than any other firm in town and you will lose price shoppers. As such, we need at least two plans. The problem with only having two packages is that the majority of people will select the lowest-priced package. If three packages are offered, the majority will move to the middle. So, we need three packages.

The challenges to this pricing strategy are:

- Introducing the new services (like valet parking)
- Restricting families to the services they paid for.

Nice resorts charge $300 to $3000 a night for a room. Regardless of what they charge for the room, the guest still pays additional to play golf, tennis, use the spa, eat in the restaurant, view movies and have a drink from the mini-bar. Staying at the resort makes all of the accommodations convenient; but there is a charge, as there should be. If a guest is not a golfer, why should they be charged additional for golf?

The same applies to a funeral home; why should a family without children pay for the use of the children's room? If the family plans to go to a restaurant for the reception, why should they have to pay for the reception room at the funeral home? In contrast, if a family does want personalization, valet parking and Internet functions, children's room or reception room, why shouldn't they be available for a fee? The only reason funeral homes didn't charge for extras in the past was that most families wanted the same thing. There didn't seem to be a reason to be restrictive.

Today, everybody wants it their way and some people are willing to pay more for it; which is why we have to learn to offer new services, even those no one has previously requested. By offering new services and products we expand the universe of potential customers and the relationship between the funeral home and their best customers is strengthened.

What Impact Will Good-Better-Best Packages Have?

On Price Shoppers: Someday most, or all funeral homes will have packages at various price points. But until then, the leaders will capture more business from price shoppers. Their basic services package (good) will be very price competitive with any discounter. But, as we know, shoppers that can afford to be discerning will select the best value package based upon their needs; not the best price.

On Pre-need: Many pre-need shoppers are looking for the best price; any pre-need counselor knows that to be true. The lowest-priced package will appeal to them; but what about their children ten years later? Will the children opt to add the personalization line item, the valet parking, and upgrade the container?

On Aftercare: One of the greatest challenges with aftercare programs is that once the widow enters the aftercare program and attends a few sessions, they never decide to stop attending the sessions. As such, two groups become four, four groups become eight, and the aftercare department grows into a very expensive day care program. Value packages could denote when aftercare services end.

- The good package would include one in-home visit following the funeral
- The better package could offer 9 weeks

- The best package could include 18 weeks or go on forever.

On Merchandise Sales: Research conducted for Wilbert Funeral Services in 1990 demonstrated that the more services the consumer purchased with cremation disposition, the better the urn purchase. Certainly, it is likely families selecting the "good" package will also purchase a lower-quality casket and outer container. But families opting for "better" and "best" will select better in keeping with the quality.

On Dignity Memorial: Many families considering affinity packages will want to compare prices for similar packages. Developing stepped priced packages will facilitate comparison and make the true value more apparent.

At-need Arrangements: One of the challenges to stepped priced packages will be that families will want to purchase the "good" package, but add some of the services available in the "better" or "best" packages. It will be difficult to hold the line, but necessary. The only choices should be "good, better, best or à la carte".

On Casket Stores: Casket stores, as a group, have not had a successful track record to date. In those rare situations where they have been successful, their success resulted from convincing consumers all are the same except for the color. Including a non-sealing casket in the "good" package will not only undermine discounters, but will also frustrate casket stores, and casket sales by cemeteries.

For that matter, include a casket range in every price category, thus making every price package a complete funeral including merchandise. This will provide the family with guidance when making a selection, and they could apply a credit against a higher-priced casket if they wish.

Personalization: Personalization requires additional manhours over and above the traditional funeral. It's well worth the effort in customer satisfaction, nonetheless, it does cost more to provide. Let's not contribute to the existing problem by including yet another "extra" service without charging for it.

Cremation: Every funeral home has a challenge of educating the consumer to their cremation choices. As such, many funeral homes offer stepped packages for cremation services starting with minimum cremation. Typically, the better cremation packages take on the form of traditional funerals offering the additional services that often accompany ground burial even though cremation consumers often select cremation to avoid the funeral. Again, the challenge is to package services consumers actually do want – not additional visitations, but the opportunity to view the cremation process to assure the returned cremated remains are actually those of their family member.

Research indicates cremation families perceive more value in personalization than do those families selecting funeral followed by burial (very likely because they are less religious). Cremation families tend to be more affluent; the restaurants and hotels they frequent offer valet parking, and they are more likely to live in condominiums thus they would see the value in reception services at the funeral home. This is exactly the group we are attempting to recapture. They will be the most responsive to "good, better, best."

Funeral homes experienced an epiphany in the '70's and 80's. Until that time, the most preferred funeral home business was the carriage trade. The carriage trade funeral homes observed the volume growth of the firms serving the mid-income communities, and the transition began. Carriage trade firms began marketing to the large middle class as the affluent consumers came to prefer cremation disposition and lower levels of services.

The largest volume funeral homes nationally are those that were most successful marketing to blue-collar consumers through the 70's and 80's. Today, the increasing number of lower-priced death care providers is victimizing those same funeral homes, to which, the owners respond, "Where is the loyalty?"

Data published by American Demographics indicate the average hourly income rate for white-collar workers approximates $22.50, and $14.20 for blue collar; or $50,000, and $35,000 respectively. As the cost of living has increased, household incomes have changed little, particularly during the recent recession and stagnant economy. Faced with tough financial decisions, consumers have been forced to shop the lowest-priced retailers. Grants was undercut by K-Mart who has been outdone by Walmart.

Mid-income consumers are shoppers by necessity. Why are we surprised they are now shopping funerals and opting for low price leaders? When the industry shifted their attention from affluent consumers to families living with strict budgets, from thought leaders to trend followers, we set in place the chain of events that has resulted in our present circumstance. Our clientele are shoppers and price watchers: to get this business, we must market and merchandise as retailers. As such, let's study how other industries market in a similar situation.

Viva Las Vegas: In the 1960's, Vegas catered to gamblers, and only gamblers. But competition from expansion in the gambling industry caused the city to market to families. Tourism has diminished with economy; Vegas and gambling responded with travel packages that combine air travel, hotel, food, and entertainment. Airline seats fill hotel beds, and create casinos. Financing for these trips is provided by credit cards.

Financing Packages Drive Auto Sales: Whenever vehicle sales slow, the car companies package the vehicle with financing programs. Rebates become down payments, three to five year, low or no interest loans are extended on select vehicles.

Packages to Go: Rooms To Go has redefined furniture buying for blue-collar families. Instead of saving for a selected piece of quality furniture, whole rooms are packaged and sold with no payments due for 14 months. (Often larger than the useful life of the furniture.)

In each of the above industries, high-priced, optional purchases have been packaged to facilitate the sale. Funerals are relatively expensive and increasingly optional. Selling funerals to the mass market will demand packaging services, merchandise, and payment terms.

Case Study: Tom Blackley, owner of the Blackley Funeral Home in Ridgefield, NJ began a one-year test of various arrangement and merchandising techniques in 2002. Over the course of a year, he experimented with various forms of arrangement tools, price lists, and cremation and funeral packages. Because this is a real world experience, some of the findings are inconclusive but interesting; others are definitive.

Initially, Mr. Blackley offered no packages, and a 2% discount for full payment at the time of arrangements. To facilitate arrangement, he employed a full-color, multiple page price list that pictured caskets, vaults, urns, facilities, and provided verbal definitions of the various services his firm provided along with prices. Mr. Blackley made 38 arrangements with a 29% cremation rate under this scenario with the following results:

Burial	Casket Sale	Cremation Sale	Overall Average
$6518	$2530	$3047	$5495

After establishing the above base, Mr. Blackley changed his full-color price list to include cremation and funeral packages. Tom offered two full-service packages, consisting of basic services of funeral director and staff, embalming, preparation for viewing, choice of a one or a two-day viewing, funeral ceremony, removal, hearse, one limousine and flower car, memorial package and casket as selected. A package discount of $250 to $900 was offered depending upon the casket selected. Of the 36 families served, ten families selected a full-service burial package, the total of the discounts was $2,800. Five families selected one of six cremation packages, ranging in price of $1,790 for a direct disposal to $6,000 for a traditional service including rental casket and a limited selection of urns. The total discount for the cremation packages was $775. All totaled, $3,575 was discounted out averaging $99 for the 36 families. Tom also required full payment at the time of arrangements, which was collected without losing a funeral. The packages created the following results:

Burial	Casket Sale	Cremation Sale	Overall Average
$6,651	$2475	$4352	$6204

Incidentally, the cremation rate dropped during this period to 20% versus 29% during the initial period. Observe the significant increase in the average cremation sale, and the impact this improvement had on the overall average for the 36 cases served during this time. Urn sales experienced a 700% increase when offered with the package.

In the third stage of the test, Mr. Blackley eliminated the price packages for burial services, discontinued use of the full-color price list, using instead a simple (but well organized) FTC required price list.

Burial	Casket Sale	Cremation Sale	Overall Average
$7550	$2,744	$3556	$6795

In the final test, the cremation rate remained around 20%, and the average sale increased, not because of the cremation packages, but because burial services were merchandised à la carte. The average cremation sale was lower, but remained significantly higher than before the cremation packages were implemented.

As mentioned above, the findings are not necessarily conclusive; whether the results were impacted by the season, or other uncontrollable factors, is impossible to determine. The impact on the average sale is sufficiently different in each scenario as to suggest that packages, certainly cremation packages, are effective merchandising tools. Interestingly, casket sales remained the same throughout the period; the increase in the sale of services had no impact on the sale price of the casket.

It is logical that cremation packages, particularly packages that include urn and casket merchandise, would increase the average cremation sale. Without the package, it is likely consumers would overlook upgrades, such as a dignified cremation container and better quality urns.

The test would seem to suggest that burial services sold better without the aid of a graphic price list. Perhaps, with the price list that included written definitions of various services, families were more inclined to focus their attention on the price of the service versus the benefit. It is reasonable to believe an effective arranger could present a service more effectively, demonstrating how the family would benefit, thus focusing the attention on the value versus the price.

The question is whether all arrangers are as effective as Mr. Blackley. A large-volume funeral firm will have fifteen to thirty-five arrangers of various levels of skill and motivation. Is it reasonable to believe all of these arrangers will effectively communicate each special service available from a funeral firm, and how the family will benefit from the service? Probably not. Although price packages for traditional funeral services might not optimize funeral services under the best-case scenario, where the arranger is skilled, talented and motivated. As such, given the skill level of most arrangers, it is likely price packages for burial services would increase the average sale as the cremation packages did for Mr. Blackley.

Conclusion: Blue-collar families perceive value in funeral services because that's how the affluent thought leaders they respected in the 1960's and 70's honored their family members. Funeral firms ignored the affluent consumer to pursue the greater volume and more profitable and less demanding middle class. Over thirty years, the cost of a funeral has come to challenge the average blue-collar household budget, causing them to try low-priced alternatives. These firms often advertise lower prices, but also, by necessity, provide a lower level of service.

Questions as to how to address this challenge abound: Can the middle-income consumer afford quality caskets and quality service? What should funeral homes be attempting to sell, lower-priced, high-eye appeal merchandise, or copper caskets?

What is the best way to present funeral home products and services, à la carte or packaged?

The future of funeral service is yet to be determined. Affluent consumers are deciding daily to opt for minimal funeral services, preferring receptions at country clubs, private halls, and churches; unattended by funeral directors. A profitable funeral business demands that arrangers become more effective event planners for middle-income consumers while also developing and packaging new and creative services for those consumers who want and can afford more.

Tom Blackley is a third generation funeral director. He is a graduate of the American Academy and McAllister Institute of funeral service in New York, N.Y. (fall graduating class of 1977). A Certified Funeral Service Practitioner, Tom is active in the community and served as president of many local organizations.

CHAPTER 15

The Cremation Challenge

There have been very few absolutes in death care industry advertising over the past twenty years simply because of all of the turmoil and transition the industry has experienced; but there have been two:

- Consumers prefer a locally-owned funeral home and advertising ownership will shift families from one funeral home to another
- Advertising cremation will always increase volume.

Contrary to traditional thinking, increasing at-need and pre-need volume is not the end-all solution to every funeral businesses challenge. In fact, increasing volume with cremation business creates a whole new series of challenges; most significant of which is that most funeral directors, including those working for low-price alternatives, don't know how to communicate with families that prefer cremation.

Funeral arrangers consider a cremation family as a "free pass." Because the family wants cremation, the funeral director doesn't feel any obligation to create a meaningful memory; they don't try to communicate the value of memorialization or services, and when challenged they simply respond "what are you going to do; they only wanted cremation?

One reason this problem persists is that the arranger is not challenged by families that prefer cremation because they assume they know everything a funeral home offers, and they are certain they don't want it.

Making productive cremation arrangements is a matter of confidence and competence; knowing what to say and when to say it. Developing confidence and competence is a matter of training. The arranger's challenge is to demonstrate the breadth of services the funeral home offers. This presentation must be done under the assumption that the consumer is not familiar with personalization as a concept or how services would be conducted or scheduled. Most importantly, the arranger must assume the family does not know how these special services contribute to a meaningful event. The more options a family learns about, the more services they are likely to choose.

Productive arrangements start with accepting that families that prefer cremation want to have a meaningful service; certainly not all, but the great majority. They are affluent and can afford whatever they want; but what they want are ideas; recommendations that will make the event special and that they will be proud to have their friends witness and participate in. Without the aid of presentation tools, a family might learn about three or four personalization and memorialization options. With presentation tools they will learn about 50 or more.

Many owners have procrastinated on training their staff so as to avoid the anticipated backlash from staff that management is changing their job from one of arranger to one of sales. Somehow owners have justified living on reduced incomes that result from thinner cremation margins as opposed to challenging arrangers to improve. Although reducing profitability is bad enough, the other side of the coin is that the most dissatisfied death care services' customers are those that have minimal services as opposed to families that select memorialization and tributes.

How Do We Sell Cremation Services?

Funeral homes devote large sections of their facilities to merchandise caskets, urns and clothing; yet make little effort to help consumers understand the varied forms of personalization available. Sales tools are fundamental and used in every business to facilitate communication with consumers. The ceilings of European churches built 1,000 years ago were painted to illustrate biblical stories. The priests would use the paintings to relate bible stories to their mostly illiterate parishioners. To sell personalization, the arranger should have tools that graphically present the services funeral homes offer.

Ask yourself, would it make you more comfortable if a funeral home offered you a warm cookie and coffee during the arrangement room? Would it be nice to have soothing music piped into the arrangement room? Would it be nice if the funeral home referred you to a good local restaurant or banquet facility, or even profiled a room where a reception could be catered onsite? Would you be more likely to spend more time in the arrangement room with the funeral directors that did all of the above? The answer to all of the above is yes, of course.

A New Twist on Cremation Societies

Cremation societies have traditionally been the nemeses of traditional funeral homes. Consumers often feel they must patronize a cremation society if cremation is their choice of disposition. Ironically, families preferring cremation have been known to telephone traditional funeral homes to inquire about visitations, wakes, funerals and memorial services after having contracted with a cremation society for crematory services assuming the funeral home could not provide cremation.

Other consumers like the idea of joining a cremation society feeling they have taken an appropriate step in locking in their preference.

Because cremation societies typically focused their advertising on low cost, minimal disposition, many funeral homes have been discouraged to advertise their cremation services with the fear that the consumer would either assume a very low price, or would simply price compare them with other alternatives.

The point is that most families preferring cremation are affluent, and can certainly afford any form of death care services. Certainly, there are some consumers who will opt only for the lowest-priced alternative; but there are a large number of cremation families willing to pay additional for the peace of mind of knowing their deceased was tended to by a well established company familiar to them.

Based upon this, an opportunity exists for funeral homes that own and operate their own crematory to create a "cremation society" using the funeral home name. For example, the Gould Cremation Society would be an operating division of the Gould Funeral Home. Incorporating the name of a well established funeral home in the cremation society name will lend credibility to the new cremation society. This is in contrast to the many cremation societies that feature the name of a state, or other local, or other generic feature. Being affiliated with a funeral home will lend credibility to the new cremation societies, support their claim of quality services, which will in turn support higher fees.

As with any cremation society, memberships should be sold in advance for a relatively low fee ($50 to $200). The benefit of membership in the society is a lower cost for cremation services compared to a non-member, retail charge for cremation at time of need. Additional benefits to membership could include discounted prices on merchandise (urns, containers, jewelry, etc.) and services (memorial services, reception room events, graveside services, etc.) at time of need.

The marketing benefit to the funeral home of starting a cremation society is that it will position the funeral home to upgrade the family to services and merchandise sales at time of need. Further, it allows the funeral home to move with society as cremation rates increase, as opposed to appearing to be in contrast with society.

Advertising for the cremation society would employ all or part of the funeral home's name; for example, the Gould Cremation Society would be a division of the Gould-Smith Funeral Home. Although the name would be similar, it is different enough for the consumer to identify the difference. In this same vein, the logo art for the cremation society name would be different from the logo art used by the funeral home. Again, the objective is for the consumer to know the society is related to the funeral home, but that it is a different entity, with its own pricing, and services. In this way, consumers will more easily understand the price differences (if any) between the cremation society and the funeral home.

Advertising media employed by the new cremation society would include television, newspaper and even billboard. Direct mail and newspaper inserts would be used to solicit memberships. The cremation society would need a new member package which would be mailed upon receipt of the membership application and fee. The package would include a membership certificate, and information regarding the cremation process and memorial options available with cremation. Ideally, members would be placed on a mailing list for a newsletter that would continue to educate the family of the many memorial options available with cremation at the funeral home and local cemeteries.

Summary: A graduate student in a masters program at the University of Houston Hilton School of Restaurant and Hotel Management Program telephoned MKJ offices recently to collect information for her thesis on funeral service personalization as a means of expanding the hotel industry into death care. She commented that hotels have to expand their business from just business travelers and brides. Think about it; chances are the hospitality industry will be successful capturing funeral business because they pride themselves on being event planners as opposed to embalmers. They want nothing to do with the deceased and will gladly leave that to the "undertaker."

As we have seen with minimal cremation, fees for disposing of human remains will not support the traditional funeral home. The argument that funeral directors did not go to embalming school to become salespeople will sound sadly prophetic when licensed people do no more than prepare bodies for visitations at hotels or transport them to crematories.

CHAPTER 16

Combinations as a Marketing Concept

Over the past thirty years, cemetery/mortuary combinations' share of the traditional funeral business on a national basis has grown from 4% to an estimated 30%. What is the appeal of this concept that is sufficiently strong enough to break consumers' patronage with traditional funeral homes?

Consumer market research conducted over the past five years indicates 43% of consumers surveyed considered combinations as more convenient in that all arrangements are handled by one individual and all services are at one location. Furthermore, 71% of consumers surveyed perceived combinations as a better value because they provide the same or better service for less.

When asked how a funeral home located on a local cemetery would impact on their funeral home preference, 29% of consumers responded it would have a strong or positive impact on their funeral home selection. Another 63% said they would consider the new option along with every other funeral home option available, and judge it on its own merit.

In other words, if the consumer was interested in the most convenient funeral home, or the funeral home providing the best service, they would consider the combination along with every other funeral home and select the firm that best met their needs. This objectivity in decision making runs contrary to many funeral directors' perceptions of strong customer loyalty.

The reality appears to be that most consumers are loyal to a funeral home as long as they feel that funeral home offers equal or better value as other available options. As a result, combinations compete very well in both at-need and pre-need.

At-need

There are several inherent advantages to the combination concept that impact on at-need selection:

- Market research indicates a new funeral home located on a cemetery will open with name awareness as strong, if not stronger, than that of the predominant stand-alone funeral home. This is very significant when one considers the annual investment funeral homes make each year in calendars, church bulletins and other name awareness advertising.

- Another critical element in the success of combinations is the perception that they represent an alternative to the traditional funeral home. Funeral homes have done such a poor job over the years in differentiating themselves that 80% of consumers see little or no difference in their funeral home options. This, in part, explains why consumers have exhibited strong loyalty to funeral homes; why bother to try another if they are all the same?

However, combinations offer what appears to be a real option. First, the funeral facility is almost always a new, modern building. This can be a very important criterion in funeral home selection when senior adults consult with their children. The "baby boomer" generation has consistently rejected everything their parents have believed. Clothing, lifestyle, personal finances and relationships have all been redefined by this generation.

Thus, when faced with a choice between a traditional funeral home with a downtown location versus a new facility located in the suburbs, many families see the advantages of the combination.

- A combination is simply a marketing concept, just like pre-need or aftercare. The only reason for building a combination is because it will help attract at-need business. As with any marketing concept, the easier it is to communicate the advantages, the more successful it will be.

- One great advantage of all of the above at-need advantages is that they are easily presented in advertising. Whether in direct mail, newspaper or television, concepts such as convenience, value and "new" are easy to relate to and understand.

Pre-Need

National research conducted in 1980 by the Batesville Casket Company indicated only a very small percent of at-need volume conducted at funeral homes had been prearranged. However, the same study indicated pre-need ownership would grow on average 25% annually. At the same time, prepaid cemetery property ownership was expected to increase an average of 40% annually.

Americans predisposition to pre-plan cemetery property before funeral services gives combinations a great sales advantage. It is generally accepted that it is easier to sell someone something when there is an established relationship than when no previous relationship existed.

This advantage bodes poorly for stand-alone funeral homes. During the period when combinations' share of the traditional market grew precipitously, pre-need sales also grew. Since 1974, 7.5 million pre-need contracts have been purchased.

Between 1992 and the year 2000, an estimated 25,000,000 additional funeral contracts will be pre-paid. If the two phenomena are related (and they most likely are), one could deduct the result of pre-need marketing during the remainder of this century to determine funeral home preferences for many years to come in the advantage of combinations.

How Funeral Homes Compete

Traditionally, funeral homes have competed on basically similar terms. Most funeral homes were locally owned and operated, and had resources similar to their competitors. The mergers and acquisitions and growth of cemetery/mortuary combinations have changed the environment in which funeral homes compete.

As a result, funeral homes must change their marketing tactics. In the past, funeral homes have committed a variety of marketing sins; but since their competitor was committing the same sins, it did not matter a great deal. These same sins today could result in significant market share shifts to combinations. They are:

1. Advertising without a plan or objective. Often duplicating the efforts of a competitor.

2. Reacting to circumstances. Some firms advertise when they have surplus cash, others advertise when they haven't had a call. In either case, the effort most likely rendered no tangible result because it lacked a consumer orientation.

3. Investing in advertising with no purpose or chance of succeeding. Specifically, church bulletins, yearbooks, team sponsorships and calendars.

4. Avoiding marketing programs which were complicated or demanded too much effort, such as aftercare or pre-need.

5. Poor timing. Advertising sporadically routinely (such as daily or weekly) can render a large portion of a budget wasted. Instead, advertising should be scheduled with consideration given to media rates, consumer lifestyles and the nature of the campaign.

When competing with a combination or any well-organized competitor, it is important to work from a plan and maintain a constant presence in the market. This does not mean running the same advertisement daily, but scheduling various public relations and advertising efforts throughout the year.

A successful strategy when competing against a combination has two elements:

- Lock in current patronage.
  - Contact current pre-paid funeral owners to remind them of their investment and advise them of their potential financial loss if they should switch.
  - Elevate public relations activities. Personal knowledge of a staff member is still a primary criterion in funeral home selection.
  - Enlist staff participation in presenting pre-need to at-need families.
  - Elevate at-need and pre-need advertising and sales efforts.
- Increase at-need base. Traditionally, funeral homes have carved out niches based upon ethnic, religious or geographic lines. When a combination opens, it must be assumed the new entity will do some, if not a lot of business. The challenge for the stand-alone funeral home is not just to compete with the combination, but to elevate their level of competition with every other funeral home in the market.

  By advertising to a larger geographic area, by being flexible in services, and by involving staff members in public relations efforts, a stand-alone funeral firm can maintain or increase volume through market share shifts even while losing some business to the combination.

Summary: The 1990's will be a decade of continuous transition for funeral service. Along with the inclusion of combinations, many smaller funeral firms will find it impossible to remain open in the face of OSHA, EPA an ADA. By the end of the century, there will be far fewer funeral facilities conducting far more funerals than the average funeral home today.

The key is to move with the transition. One way to accomplish this is to take advantage of proven methods for increasing volume, such as acquisition, merger, pre-need, aftercare, and public relations, along with other forms of marketing.

CHAPTER 17

Cooperative Marketing: A Response to Today's Changing Consumer

Research studies conducted by MKJ Marketing over the past two years have included a survey question which asks the respondent which of eight special services a funeral home could offer, would be most important to them. Consistently ranked either number 2 or 3, (behind personalization) is being able to arrange monuments, flowers and cemetery property while making funeral arrangements.

Traditionally, convenience was defined as having the closest location to the consumer.

- Banks built 2500 sq. ft. branch banks everyfive miles;
- Major intersections had a gas station and convenience store on at least three of four corners;
- Hospitals built neighborhood clinics.

The re-definition of convenience began with the Internet, with every service and product being as near as your computer. Even with this, the large pharmacy retailers race to tear down service stations and banks to build 10,000 sq. ft. retail centers and drug stores on every corner. Why the demand for so many new retail centers? Because, following the .com melt down, convenience now means accomplishing as many tasks as possible at one place.

Surveys conducted for retailers indicate consumers will pay up to 15% more for better service; and the greatest service is saving the customer time.

Applying this to death services is simple; many funeral homes offer monument and flower selections, cremation services (often from their own crematory on the premises), and other conveniences. A mortuary/cemetery's inherent advantage is the convenience of all services at one location. But is that enough?

Often, managers overlook the most obvious marketing advantages. Issues which should be included in a business's advertising rotation are omitted simply because management underestimates its significance to the consumer. Case in point: The drug store industry has built hundreds of large pharmacy/retail centers on prime real estate all over the country with the apparent strategy of making it convenient for shoppers to run in, make their purchase, and run out. The profit stream is derived from the higher prices charged versus grocery stores and discount retailers for the same products.

Management at one such chain concluded that they could increase the average sale by holding the customer in the store longer; to accomplish this they set about creating ways to keep shoppers in the stores longer. Will this increase the average sale, or simply cause customers to shop elsewhere?

As ridiculous as this example seems, let's examine some of the convoluted logic pervasive in funeral service:

- The arrangement session is the best opportunity to present the value of the funeral and to communicate the options available to families. Instead, arrangers spend time completing government mortality forms and accomplishing mundane administrative functions which could be better accomplished by administrative clerks, or by the family alone.

- Funeral homes employ livery services for first call as opposed to taking the opportunity to begin building a personal relationship with the family and to inform the family of the type of information required when making arrangements.

- Families preferring cremation disposition represent the industries' best opportunity to increase the average sale; so many funeral firms assign the least informed arranger to make cremation arrangements.

- Personalized funerals enhance the customer's satisfaction with the funeral, but few funeral homes make the tools available to arrangers to effectively communicate how a funeral can be customized to meet the family's needs.

- Pre-need is the ultimate convenience, but most funeral homes are still without a pre-need counselor.

- Video tributes are wonderful, inexpensive ways to personalize a funeral, but most funeral homes fail to make the service available.
- Most combinations aggressively advertise pre-need cemetery sales, but seldom effectively build their brand image as a convenient alternative to stand-alone funeral homes and cemeteries.
- Pre-need counselors from combinations are often prohibited from representing both the cemetery and funeral services. The rationale that independent sales forces will generate greater sales ignores the consumer's priority of making all decisions with one individual at one time.
- Family car drivers are often asked about pre-need; yet few firms provide them with the necessary information to make an intelligent response.
- The best opportunity for growing volume is to reach people without an established funeral home preference; often newcomers to a community. Instead of employing media that effectively reaches newcomers, funeral homes advertise on the obituary page of the newspaper that is almost never read by new residents.
- Many funeral homes have a staff dedicated to pre-need sales, but almost none have an arranger dedicated to cremation arrangements.

Perhaps the most obvious marketing opportunity in the death services industry would be cooperative marketing initiatives by independent funeral homes and cemeteries. Even states which prohibit ownership of funeral homes and cemeteries by one entity would allow two independent companies to jointly advertise and pre-sell their services. A consumer familiar with one of the cooperating companies would consider the joint advertising campaign as a testimonial for the other business.

Exchanging a cemetery's list of property holders for names and addresses of families previously served by a funeral home may sound like a radical idea; but list sharing is pervasive in other industries. Certainly, it would be appropriate for both sides of the agreement to insist on approving copy for any correspondence mailed to families on their respective lists.

Cooperation could enhance common marketing challenges; if adopted earlier enough, it may have been an effective means of retarding the growth of cremation. That opportunity may be lost now, but others exist. For example, it is critical for the death services industry to promulgate personalization. Many consumers simply do not relate to the traditional religious-based funeral service. Certainly, personalization would make more sense to consumers if they saw a common theme carried out from the funeral service, the casket, the vault, the graveside service, the monument and flowers. Accomplishing this is simply a matter of looking beyond the past and focusing on common objectives.

CHAPTER 18

The Toughest Concept to Accept in Funeral Service: Not All Business Is Good for Business.

It's too easy to say funeral business is unlike any other business. It takes more thought to see how funeral service is actually very similar to other businesses; once arriving at that conclusion, the ambiguities of funeral service marketing fade and the priorities become more clear.

Because the industry has always measured success by comparing "calls," the long-established objective has been to attract greater volume. One look at funeral service on the west coast provides all the evidence one needs to see the fallacy of focusing on volume instead of quality.

So how does a funeral home develop a clientele of quality business versus volume? To a great extent, this process has already begun with the market segmentation resulting from the growth of low-cost alternative death services. Nonetheless, most funeral businesses continue to invest too much time focusing on volume and too little time focusing on quality. So the question remains; how do we increase the average sale?

In simple terms, funeral homes must be willing to walk away from some business.

Is it any wonder the most affluent, exclusive segment of the U.S. population, the group most financially able to afford our best products and services, have become disinterested in traditional funeral services? From the 1950's through the 80's they saw themselves paying premium prices for fundamentally the same service funeral homes made available to others for far less. Not wanting to pay more for what others received for less, the most affluent now represent the market for minimal cremation services, or memorial services without the assistance of a funeral director.

This situation is exacerbated by the profession's tradition of serving the indigent with honor. When a family is without financial resources, funeral homes graciously offer to provide a funeral service for whatever the county is willing to pay for indigent care.

Fine restaurants feel no obligation to feed the indigent. Fine hotels don't offer rooms to the homeless. Why should funeral homes serve the indigent? And if funeral homes do serve those unable to pay, why should that service include use of facilities, caskets, outer containers, transportation to the cemetery and in-ground interment? Why shouldn't the indigent be served by minimal cremation services? What is the honor to a family able to pay to use the same facilities as society's lowest class? There is none.

Creating a "Scarcity Issue"

The scarcer something is, the more people are willing to pay for it. Antiques cost more than fine quality, new furniture. Collectible vehicles cost more today than when they were new. An old baseball card is more valuable than the thousands sold everyday with bubblegum. When a business creates a scarcity of something people want, they can charge more for it; mahogany caskets cost more than oak, not because it's more beautiful, but because it is more scarce.

What about funeral home services are scarce? For busy funeral homes, the number of funerals conducted in the morning could be considered a scarcity. Also, the attendance by a particular funeral director could be considered a commodity of limited availability. The use of a particular visitation room, Saturday or Sunday funerals, or the use of a particularly beautiful chapel could all justify a higher service charge.

Communicating Value

The first challenge is to create elements of value and to charge for them appropriately. The next challenge is to sell them. The funeral home mantra for generations relative to advertising was to simply "keep their name out there." Research indicates consumers can name 80% of the funeral homes serving their community. As such, the challenge is not keeping one's name in front of the public; instead it is to present the special values the funeral home offers.

Advertising elements of value is one means of selling; others are through the pre-need sales counselors, funeral directors, and public relations efforts. How much time do owners and managers invest instructing their staff in the value difference offered by their firm?

Building Fences

Strategically, there must be a clear and visible difference in death care services if those who are willing and able to purchase the very best are to continue to do so. The first step in creating this clear difference is a willingness to walk away from business. Secondly, there must be a methodology in place to allow the firm to select its customers without prejudice. By rejecting some business, businesses strengthen their relationship with their very best customers.

Whenever funeral home owners discuss pricing, they become uncomfortable with the concept of charging one customer more than another, even when they provide additional value to the higher paying family. The discomfort is no doubt related to a code of ethics to treat every family with dignity. Treating the deceased with dignity is not the same as giving away services and merchandise.

Balancing what consumers want with what they will tolerate is the defining principle of discounting, whether in food service, grocery stores, air travel, or funeral service. No other profession, industry, or business has the level of difficulty appreciating this simple but vital foundation of successful business.

Automotive companies have no difficulty leaving luxury items off their basic products in order to hold down the price. Neither do hotels, hospitals, doctors, dentists, or attorneys. Most businesses accomplish this by "building fences." The fences are the barriers that define when one level of service stops and the next begins. If you want to buy your airline ticket at the last moment, it'll cost you more than if you purchased it months in advance. If you want to watch the sun fall from a restaurant terrace, it costs more than lunch at the same table.

Why should prices be consistent throughout a funeral firm when services are delivered from multiple facilities? A downtown facility built in 1910 has a very different cost basis than a new, single story facility located convenient to the suburbs, offering modern comforts and accommodations.

Should the fee charged for the use of an older hearse or family car, be the same as charged for a brand new vehicle?

Should cremation services conducted by the funeral home, on funeral home property, cost the same as that of a competitor who uses a commercial crematory located in another county? More importantly, how much more will consumers pay to know the job was conducted by the funeral home they selected, with their own equipment versus an unknown third party?

How many people would select a higher level of service if they knew it included admission to a special grief seminar or counseling session for their family following the services? Or a special grief counseling service conducted during the holidays, hosted by their funeral director and moderated by a local licensed counselor?

Online services such as a Remembrance Registry and LifeLegacy can be packaged as additional benefits exclusive to the highest-priced service option. Or separate the two with Remembrance Registry alone in the mid-point package, and the two together in the highest-priced package.

Personalized funerals certainly cost more to conduct, shouldn't the elements of personalization be packaged at a higher price than a more typical service?

By loading special services and products into price brackets, funeral homes would be able to establish new levels of services available only to those willing to pay more. A simple truth of pricing:

- When people have only two options, the majority will select the lowest priced.
- When they have three choices, the majority will move to the middle.

Summary: An average strategy with great execution is far more productive than a great strategy with average execution. Small businesses become moribund when implementing new strategies because of fear their plan is not perfect.

Instead of focusing on the details of the strategy, focus more on the day-to-day implementation. Study what you are saying to your community through your advertising; is it telling your story as it should be presented, or are you simply buying space in the newspaper?

Does your staff buy into your pricing strategy and communicate the value? There have been amazing technological advancements in every segment of American life. No one would consider using a computer based upon 1980's technology, or control their home's climate with a 1960's era heating/air conditioning unit. Yet everyday, funeral directors recommend burial vaults designed in the 1960's to families as "all they need." Anyone who recommends forty-year old technology in a product is very likely unprepared or unable to present the quality difference between one funeral home and another.

Begin by identifying those elements of your services, facilities, cars, merchandise, etc. that consumers place the most value in. Then investigate the availability of products and services available to the industry your firm doesn't presently offer. This process is referred to as dispersion analysis.

Then develop bundles of services and products to create various price levels; good, better and best. Then price accordingly. Naming the packages can be a little tricky; as we have learned in funeral service, few families consider themselves worthy of the "best." As such, the highest-valued bundle might be called the "traditional;" the second level the "simple" service, and the lowest price the "basic."

Train staff to present the packages. First, they listen to what the family wants or needs. A family with relatives all over the country would be interested in the Remembrance Registry as a means of allowing family and friends to contribute to the service through their email correspondence. Punctuating this special benefit offered exclusively at the highest price point will give the family reason to move up.

Provide sales tools to present the various packages, including a binder with pictures of families working together to create a personalized funeral. Photos of services conducted in a more decorative or historic chapel versus a plainer room should be utilized.

Make these added features the subject of newspaper and television advertising as a means of influencing funeral home selection.

Cynics will argue it's impossible to sell packages at higher prices; consumers simply don't care. Yet the same consumers buy up in every other area of their personal spending, and funeral service is no different.

CHAPTER 19

Making Better Decisions Is a Matter of Having Better Information

We have entered the Super Bowl season of market research. Every four years, American voters' most intimate social and political thoughts are picked and studied as politicians develop platforms, positions and talking points. This is where the period of peak demand for research services, but also where theory and practical application meet. Politicians will pay whatever is necessary for new research techniques that will reveal data competitors will not have. The success of these ideas, filter into commercial applications after they have been proven in the political arena.

Tightening profit margins in funeral service are causing funeral businesses of all sizes to develop strategic plans. Long term and short term plans that involve succession planning with younger generations acquiring family businesses, advertising budgets, acquisition and sale of businesses or properties. All are important, perhaps life changing, decisions.

Planners meet with family members to assist in this process, and they ask important questions; what is your market share, why do people use your firm versus competitors, and vice versa? Are your location, facility, staff, prices, services, name awareness, image, and pre-need competitive? Too often these questions are answered based upon perceptions, or misperceptions, family members have held for generations, starting with great, great granddaddy.

Too often these marketing plans simply reinforce existing assumptions. Owners and managers will assume that everyone believes like they do about services, competitors, prices and facilities. The reality is without some source of objective data, developing a long-term strategy without market research is like getting a physical without a blood test.

How Market Research Contributes to Planning

The cost of marketing-by-assumption can be enormously high, particularly when an organized market profile study can easily prevent mistakes. When people know rather than assume they will make significantly better decisions. Market research will pinpoint consumer groups who may not be aware of your funeral firm or could be attracted to patronize a particular funeral home if they were made aware of the special services provided, such as on-site crematories, reception and children's rooms. Creating advertising that will impact decision making is far easier once the consumer's hot buttons have been identified.

Another benefit of a market analysis for existing facilities is to determine the importance of certain criteria in the selection of a funeral home. In some regions, consumers are very familiar with their funeral home options and are likely to refer to their own experience when selecting a funeral home. But, in a highly mobile society where as much as 20% of residents relocate annually, there are many consumers with no local funeral home experience upon which to base a decision. In these cases, it is important to have an understanding of the role the clergy, yellow pages, Internet, print and broadcast media advertising play in funeral home selection.

Using Market Research to Plan New Facilities and Acquisitions

The tradition of funeral service is to take uncalculated risk when expanding or building a new funeral facility. Through pure tenacity on the part of owner/operators, many of the nation's newer funeral homes have remained open when business volume did not merit the cost. Most of these unnecessary and expensive facilities could have been avoided by a moderate investment in consumer market research.

Many funeral homes have been built because an operator in a neighboring community felt the funeral homes in the area did not provide quality services, or their facilities were inadequate. These assumptions ignore a fundamental element of funeral service: that funeral business, like many other businesses, is more about personal relationships than any other single factor. Judging a funeral business by its building or service is the same as judging a book by its cover. Typically, the existing firms in an area meet the local clientele's expectations. It can take years for a new facility to build volume simply because residents like the owners of a competitive firm, regardless of the building or prices.

A market research study during the planning stages of a new facility will reveal information about prospective consumers by focusing on what they really want from a funeral home; what factors they consider when selecting a funeral home. Accurate and specific consumer attitudinal information about a prospective trade area can predict at-need volume and assist funeral home owners and managers in determining the demand for a particular facility. Fundamental questions like location, building design and size can be answered.

Over the past five years, only one of every two clients conducting a prospective trade area study has decided to move ahead with new facilities. This means that half of the time owners that were prepared to invest millions of dollars in new facilities were dissuaded from moving ahead based upon information they learned from market research, such as:

- What influences a family to choose one funeral home over another?
- What families see as assets and liabilities of one facility versus another?
- The proportion of consumers owning a pre-paid funeral.
- The proportion of families who are unsure as to which funeral facility they will patronize.
- Sources used to select a funeral home.
- Present and projected volume of deaths in an area.
- Demographics, i.e., age, income, length of residence.

Prior to purchasing property for a new facility, research will indicate whether or not there is sufficient at-need volume to support a proposed facility or if one site would be more productive than another. By understanding the consumer's priorities, marketing efforts are made more efficient and productive. A funeral firm can be assessed in terms of:

- How well known and liked is the staff by local consumers?
- How does the firm's reputation compare to that of others in the area?
- Does the firm meet the consumers' expectations as far as flexible costs and services?

- Is the firm associated with one religious group more than another?
- Do consumers see value in special services such as aftercare, pre-need or rental caskets?

Making Market Research Work

There are many methods for collecting consumer data, and each was developed to meet a specific need. Focus groups are becoming increasingly common in funeral service as management teams need qualitative data that cannot be ascertained through telephone interviews. Focus groups bring residents of your community together to discuss issues important to you; such as special services, the consumer's understanding of cremation, memorialization with cremation, columbarium niches, cremation scattering options in cemeteries, and other options.

Most funeral home research needs are quantitative in nature, meaning a large number of respondents must be surveyed. Quantitative research answers fundamental questions such as why one firm is preferred over another, why is volume down, what do consumers like about one firm, versus another, and what are the opportunities for market share gains.

It's very easy to commission a research study that produces 200 pages of charts and graphs but no practical information, no recommendations or direction upon which to base a decision. One funeral home owner was convinced to conduct a mail-out survey study. The questionnaire was sent to adult residents of his community; of which only 12 were returned, six of which were clergy members. A thick report was produced, which obviously had no value whatsoever at reporting what the community thought about the local funeral homes.

Market research should be used to investigate specific rather than general issues. For example, the most common question business people will ask is "Why do consumers do what they do?" Determining "why" is deceptively difficult. When people are asked direct questions about what they do, they are inclined to answer with rationalizations rather than reasons because people want other people to believe they are reasonable. So, they search for ways to rationalize their behavior and make their actions acceptable to others. Answering "why" is not a realistic research objective; but knowing what consumers will do meets our needs as marketers. Market research should answer specific questions that contribute to specific decisions rather than a long list of generalizations:

"Is there a market for this new facility?"

"How much can we charge for our services?"

"How much opportunity is there in the market for volume growth?"

"What do I have to do to grow this business?"

"How is my pre-need program doing compared to others in this market?"

Involve all individuals with responsible positions within the firm to recommend issues that should be investigated by the research. Whether at-need, pre-need, or family follow-up, there will be important questions which, when answered, will allow this individual to better perform and may apprise the rest of the organization of special opportunities.

Make a commitment to accept the results of the research study even when they run contrary to held beliefs. The marketplace is full of misinformation. Consumers believe things to be true that you may know to be false. This does not mean the survey is wrong; rather, someone is misinformed. One of the greatest contributions of a market profile study is to reveal areas of misinformation so as to allow managers to make their promotion and advertising more effective and productive by realigning perceptions.

Conclusion

The dynamics of a sophisticated and diverse consumer market combined with high interest rates and construction costs and a fiercely competitive marketplace make a careful marketing plan for prospective or existing funeral facilities essential for success.

Every manager and owner in the funeral industry should be alert for ways to reduce the risks of a new facility and for ways to generate greater volume at existing facilities. As many funeral professionals have stated, "It costs too much today to make mistakes." To avoid that end, market research can be a most helpful tool.

Remember, marketing-by-assumption leaves open the possibility that it may be you who is misinformed and not the consumer.

Market Research Case Studies:

Having conducted 600 market research studies and moderated hundreds of focus groups and test panels for funeral homes, cemeteries and death care industry vendors, the most amazing phenomena is to observe an intelligent business manager make a business decision with significant long-term implications in direct contradiction to hard research data. It's impossible to list all of the instances when this has occurred, but the following are typical:

A Midwest funeral home owner commissioned a research study to determine the prospects for a new funeral home in a relatively large city. The research data demonstrated that the client already pulled most of the business from this area and because the population was so young and transient, the number of deaths from the area would not increase for many years. The client chose to proceed with the new facility under the rationale that he had two sons and wanted each to have their own business. The client was apprised that what he was actually doing was digging an expensive hole from which his son would spend the rest of his career trying to emerge, but the facility was built. Fifteen years later it has yet to conduct a sufficient number of calls annually to meet the overhead cost.

A major industry vendor was considering a personalization product to replace a more generic standard product that all funeral homes use. The proposed product had merit as it was more attractive, but the nature of the product made it very cumbersome for funeral homes, as it would require them to carry extensive inventory. The client observed two focus groups of funeral directors, each of which made it very clear they would not purchase the product because of the need for a large inventory and because the product is so specific it limited the opportunities for use. Nonetheless, the client ignored the research finding and pursued the product. The product failed miserably and contributed to the president's termination.

- A funeral home client in a Midwestern city had not initiated a pre-need marketing effort even as competitors experienced good success with their individual efforts. The client conducted a research study that clearly demonstrated that the competition was gaining market share among younger adults (age 55+) primarily through their pre-need sales efforts. The research also demonstrated that consumers did not believe the client offered pre-need and had reluctantly shifted their preference to other firms that did offer pre-need. As the age 55+ consumers aged into the age 65+ generation, the client funeral home has steadily lost market share among families preferring traditional burial and now has a far higher cremation rate than the competition. The very high cremation rate has resulted in lower profit margins, and the owners have lost tremendous equity as the acquisition value of the firm has declined.

- Funeral home owners often consider building a new funeral home too near a major competitor under the assumption that being located near a major competitor is a good strategy for pulling business from the competitor. Research and experience has demonstrated just the opposite. Consumers need a good reason to change their funeral home preference from one firm to another, and simply locating near their preferred funeral home is not good enough. A market research study was suggested to a client that had intentions to do exactly the above. The research was conducted and the results demonstrated that a new facility in another area of town would be far more successful. Nonetheless the client built the new facility on property near the competitor. Today that facility is law offices.

- A funeral business has two facilities that operate with similar, but different names. One of the facilities has never performed as well as the other. The owner commissioned a research study to determine why one building was so much more successful then the other. The results demonstrated that consumers did not know the two buildings were owned by the same company and held negative image perceptions of the less successful facility. The solution was obvious; change the name of the less successful facility to reflect the common ownership and promote the two facilities under one name. Management was reticent to drop the heritage names associated with the underperforming facility, and to date, the facility continues to underperform.

- A large manufacturing company commissioned test panels to create a merchandising system that would sell more profitable products. The research results dramatically indicated that the product line was too broad and that sales would improve by deleting lower-end products, implementing a "good, better, best" merchandising strategy, and using a presentation book or computer-based presentation as opposed to the current selection room merchandising strategy. Although investing in excess of $100,000 in the study, the results were never implemented; product mix continues to be the company's primary challenge.

Perhaps the same mentality explains why so many funeral homes and cemeteries pursue courses that run contrary not only to research findings, but empirical data as well.

- Funeral businesses nationally have installed reception rooms with outstanding success when funeral arrangers are trained to present their catering services, yet the great majority of funeral homes fail to take advantage of this obvious opportunity.

- Funeral home profits are declining precipitously from cremation, but so few firms are implementing arrangement room strategies such as packaging and presentation systems, that have proven to increase sales and customer satisfaction.

- Research indicates 80% of consumers that want burial already own cemetery space. The objective of cemetery advertising should be to create a demand for cemetery memorialization, such as cremation niches.

- There are too many funeral homes in the U.S.; as a result weaker firms are becoming financially desperate. Because desperate people take desperate risks, pre-need and other financial scandals are rampant in the death care industry. There is an obvious need for legislation to protect the consumer from unscrupulous funeral home and cemetery operators, but the state and national associations have failed to take a proactive position by recommending regulation that could preclude the actions of a few from undermining the public's confidence in all death care businesses while also protecting the public.

- Local ownership has been the most successful advertising strategy ever implemented in the funeral home industry at shifting business from one funeral home to another. In fact, local ownership advertising is one of the main reasons the corporations are selling off isolated facilities where they are at a competitive disadvantage with locally-owned firms in deference to markets where corporate-operated funeral homes dominate. Yet, independent funeral homes have convinced themselves consumers no longer care about ownership because they don't hear them talk about it anymore. It is so apparent that consumers considered ownership important when advertising informed them of the local versus corporate issue. Consumers learn the issues they should consider through advertising, so your advertising must raise the issues you want consumers to consider important; not the other way around.

Summary: Research is a good investment when management is willing to consider the findings when making decisions. Marketing succeeds when we take a holistic perspective of our business, meaning we consider all of the influences that impact our business.

Research Fallacies

Market research has become more relevant to small businesses in recent years as the cost of facilities, advertising and staff has increased. In the 1950's through 1970's a licensed funeral director could start a funeral business in the family house and work at other jobs while the funeral business got started. But that strategy is no longer viable as commercial standards are now applied to funeral facilities, and the cost demands the facility pay for itself early on. Also, banks and lending institutions as well as private investors are more likely to make loans to a new business if they have confidence their investment will be repaid by a going concern and a well conducted research study can give them that confidence.

But what kind of research, and who should you commission to conduct a research study? The theme for a series of jewelry store advertisements was, "If you don't know jewelry, then you had better know your jeweler." The implication being that without knowledge of diamonds and gold, it was dangerous to buy jewelry if you don't know the person you're buying it from. The same applies to research; like jewelry everyone knows something about research, but is it enough to know what is needed to make your investment in information pay off?

The most common mistake is investing in the wrong kind of research. Clients love focus group research because they can observe the data collection while it's in progress. What makes it even more entertaining is that they get to observe from behind the one-way mirror. Focus groups can be very productive at collecting detailed and in depth information regarding a product or service, particularly a product or service the consumer is unfamiliar with.

Many death care industry vendors will commission focus group research when introducing new grief products to be sold through funeral homes. Focus group research is very good at identifying the objections funeral directors will encounter when they present a new product to a family. It can also provide guidance relative to pricing and advertising strategies. Many start-up discount funeral services have invested in focus group research to determine what elements of the traditional funeral service can be eliminated and still deliver something of value to the family.

Another form of qualitative research is one-on-one interviews. Again, the information generated is high quality because the researcher can ask as many questions as needed to learn the deep seeded attitudes that would not surface in a telephone interview or even in a focus group.

The shortcoming of qualitative research is that it cannot be used for making projections or predictions such as how many families will use a new funeral home or will families continue to use a family-owned funeral business if it is acquired by another company and the original family is no longer involved. To make projections as to what people will do in the future, it is necessary to collect data from a large number of people, referred to as a statistical universe.

Quantitative data can be collected in any manner of ways; Internet-based surveys, mailed out surveys and telephone interviews. Internet surveys are productive when the sample cannot be reached by telephone, which is becoming increasingly common as many people no longer have a household telephone and sample lists can not be ascertained with reliable cell phone numbers. MKJ recently conducted a research study of young adults 18 through 29, many of which were college students. College students are particularly difficult to sample because they often do not live at home.

Mailed out surveys are seldom used anymore, and really have not been in extensive use for the past twenty years as consumers became less and less inclined to return the completed surveys. When the surveys are returned, they are often only partially completed, and typically only come from respondents that either love or hate the subject business or product.

A funeral home commissioned a local research company to conduct a mailed out survey for him. Several thousand surveys were mailed out to households in the community; fewer than twenty were returned, and about half came from clergy. Obviously the data collection was a failure; but to add insult to injury, the research firm created a research report based upon a negligible response. The client should have refused to pay for this sham, but you know funeral directors are nice guys, and sooner or later the owner of that local research business will have a death in the family.

When telephone lists are available, as they are for older residents (age 45+), telephone research continues to be considered the most reliable form of data collection. This is particularly true when the subject of the study is something of interest to the respondents, which is the case with funeral service. Because the subject of the study is local businesses, and often involve people they know, the respondents are very inclined to remain on the telephone with the interviewer until the questionnaire is completed. Certainly, the length of the interview is a factor; MKJ's experience is consumers will tolerate an interview up to 20 minutes in duration. After that it's hard to keep them on the line.

A marketing company in funeral service in the 1970's conducted what they referred to as "thought leader" research. The owner of the marketing firm would visit the client's town to interview as many "thought leaders" in the form of clergy, politicians, police, attorneys, etc., as he could contact in a one or two day period. From this data he would develop a report.

"Validity" is a research term that measures whether the information generated from a research study actually relates to the questions the research was intended to answer. Ask yourself, how many politicians and civil servants are actually going to make critical comments about a local business to a complete stranger? And even if they did, how significant would the data be? Politicians have no more funerals than any other family, and their criteria in selecting a funeral home is likely to be completely irrelevant to the typical resident in the community. This data has no "validity" as it cannot tell the client why families select their funeral home and why they don't. It can not report how much market share can be gained or how to go about getting it. Basically, the report is just words on paper with little or no value.

Amazingly, research based upon clergy comments have returned to funeral service. At a time when church attendance is at an all time low, many protestant churches conduct their own funeral services, and few clergy actually recommend any funeral home even when asked by a parishioner, a company is conducting research by interviewing clergy. The information collected is totally worthless which is very dangerous since research information is collected to assist in decision making. If bad or erroneous information is dressed up in a well written report it can appear to be valid.

"Reliability" is an important issue in research as it refers to the ability of a research study to create the same results if the study was repeated. The point being that a research study that created different results every time it was conducted has little value.

Collecting reliable data can be expensive. Clients often need national-based data; for example, if a casket or vault company wanted to improve its in-funeral home merchandising system, that data would have to be collected from around the country. Test panels are often used to collect data as to how one merchandising system would fare versus another; for instance, will families purchase better quality merchandise if presented with actual products, product models, photographs on computers or books. The problem is that data collected in Charlotte will not reflect what will happen in California; so the test panels must be conducted in selected cities where the collected data will reflect the opinions of many people within a region.

Because research can be expensive, college business departments will conduct market research for local businesses, particularly focus group sessions and mailed out surveys at a reduced cost. This sounds great because the professor can use student labor for the cost of pizzas. Certainly the experience is valuable to the students involved in the process, but the question is this: Are you willing to make a significant investment based upon information derived from a school project? Remember, the student's objective is to get a good grade, not to create valuable information. How do you know the interviews were even conducted; maybe the student simply completed the questionnaires in his dorm room without talking to respondents. It's for this reason real research firms audio record every interview and conduct quality control "call backs" to confirm the information reported by the interviewer.

Another fallacy is that the research report will give definitive directions as to right and wrong decisions. It won't. The research report is created by a research analyst; the analyst is a research specialist that knows how to conduct a valid and reliable research study. The analyst creates questions for the questionnaire, determines how many respondents are necessary given the total population. The analyst assures quality control throughout the research project, but the analyst will likely not be knowledgeable about the client's business.

The research report simply tells how the respondents answered questions posed to them, typically with charts and graphs. What that data means and how it is used is the work of marketers. Large companies have marketing people on staff to interpret research data; small businesses typically do not. Small business owners don't want charts and graphs; they want reliable direction for their business; that's why it is important to employ a marketing firm (particularly one that specializes in your business) when conducting research as opposed to a market research firm that conducts the study but is not responsible for putting the information to work.

Summary: The tradition in funeral service is for families to invest millions of dollars to build a new funeral facility based upon the faith and hope that families will select the firm when a death occurs. Consider how many funeral facilities have been built to conduct 300 cases annually but have a volume of 150 or less. These mistakes cost families thousands of dollars every month for decades, and the debt is often passed on to the younger generation, or inhibit the sale of the business.

Given the transition the funeral business is experiencing based upon changing consumer attitudes and the declining profit margins on funeral service, it is simply irresponsible to make a large financial commitment without valid and reliable research data.

CHAPTER 20

Thinking Within the Box

The most common business cliché over the past decade is "thinking outside the box." Of course, this phrase has special implications in the death care industry, but let's examine it from a general marketing perspective and avoid the funeral-related pun for the moment.

Thinking outside the box relates to the idea of changing the ways things have been done in the past, which on the surface sounds like a good formula for improvement. But too often, it is simply change for change sake, which fails to get us any closer to where we want to go. For example, thinking outside the box is often the justification for changing the color of letterhead or creating a new logo. Sure, it's different, but is it better and will it actually accomplish desirable results?

Instead of thinking outside the box, let's open the box and consider its contents. Linda Rynick, in her book, "Rubies in the Orchard" (an outstanding read that I highly recommend; you will be amazed with this woman's marketing accomplishments,) demonstrates how the first step in marketing any product or service is to identify that product's intrinsic values – the core factors of the product that attracted consumers to the product in the first place. When we think outside the box, we are actually pulling ourselves away from these core factors in an effort to identify new values, often where they don't exist.

An example of this in death care would be the current interest many funeral directors have in pet cremation. By thinking outside the box it has been concluded that by soliciting pet cremation business from veterinarians, funeral directors are establishing better relationships with families which will result in future business when they experience a death in their human family. Perhaps this will occur, but it is just as likely the family will be appreciative of the job you did on their pet and return to the funeral home their family has patronized in the past.

The funeral home business model is not based upon disposition of the dead; the funeral business is about ceremony and events that bring people together. Disposition of human remains can be accomplished very inexpensively and at a cost that will not support the maintenance of even half of the nation's 22,000 funeral homes. Promulgating the perception that funeral directors are about disposition does not promote the funeral profession; in fact it detracts from the concept that ceremony, events and memorials are necessary.

Again, let's open the box and examine the contents for direction relative to pets and death. If the funeral profession is based upon ceremony, events and memorials, is there a better strategy or business model which would allow the funeral director to participate in this area of business without diminishing the funeral director's role in society? Many funeral homes are located in downtown shopping areas. Often these facilities have available floor space which could be used to merchandise pet grief products. Even if this cannot be accomplished in the funeral home premises, it can certainly be accommodated on the funeral home Web site.

Remember this, not all pet loss occurs at the veterinarian's office. Pets go missing everyday when they stray from the backyard, or are killed in traffic away from the family's home. There is not always a corpse to dispose of; but the grief will always be there. Why not promote grief products that memorialize the missing pet?

Another perspective can be gained from the automobile industry. General Motors is just emerging from bankruptcy; a perfect opportunity to begin fresh, with new ways of doing business. Prior to the 1980's, thinking inside the box, GM and Ford designed and manufactured their own vehicles. In the 1980's and 90's they were thinking outside the box when they decided to import small cars manufactured in Korea and other countries and re-badge them as Chevrolets. Thinking outside the box resulted in some of the greatest failures in automotive marketing. The vehicles did not look right to the American buyer, and did not offer the quality functions we consider important.

Thinking inside the box, domestic auto companies should focus on designing small cars for the American public, and it can be done. Look at the popularity of smaller vehicles such as the BMW 100 and 300 line, Lexus IS 250, and Infiniti G35; all big selling, relatively small cars. GM simply cannot bring itself to design quality smaller cars and this huge blind spot has cost them at least one whole generation of car buyers, if not two or three.

Applying this thought to funeral service, thinking outside the box has resulted in owners employing general managers to run their businesses and then they wonder why their profit margins are so low. Even the worse owner/manager will be more cost efficient than one of the better general managers; sure you'll make some mistakes, but will you make enough mistakes to offset the six figure salary paid to the general manager?

Thinking outside the box, many funeral home owners are attempting to enter the casket business by importing Chinese caskets. There is an ongoing dialogue as to whether funeral homes realize greater profit from imports after the cost of money, warehousing, additional labor, delays in shipping, delivery trucks and other costs. But one thing most Chinese casket proponents agree on is that the greatest profits are derived from the higher-end caskets versus the lower-end and mid-level units, and this is because they sell the higher-end product at a cost comparable to an American-made casket.

Given the way American culture is going, life after this recession will be very different than it was in the 1990's. Americans will have to lead simpler lives with fewer excesses. High-end casket sales are already in steep decline, much faster than can be accounted for by increases in cremation. The reality is Chinese manufacturers will lose their interest in the American casket business very quickly when they realize how few high-end caskets are sold over here and that they cannot beat the prices American casket companies charge for the low-end units. Chinese caskets will prove to be a blip in the funeral industry history books just like Gulf Western's venture into death care back in the early 1980's.

Thinking inside the box, funeral home owners should be working day and night to deliver more meaningful services. Families don't have funerals to buy caskets; they have funerals to meet emotional needs, and we seem to be getting further and further away from that every year. How can we get more people at funerals, how can we get family members more involved in the ceremony other than speaking in public, which is perennially Americans' greatest fear? How can we make the funeral home environment a more comfortable and accommodating facility, and how can we make the whole process more environmentally sensitive?

CHAPTER 21

A Declining Economy Creates Opportunities for Businesses that Do Things Differently

Auto companies of every ilk are suffering from the world's economic downturn. New car sales are touching all time lows, and forget about trucks and large SUV's. Some dealers have actually stopped accepting SUV's and trucks as trade-ins. A recent Wall Street Journal article discussed the possibility of Chrysler and General Motors merging in an effort to limit the number of layoffs and the devastation massive layoffs would have on the already desperate job situations in Detroit and Michigan.

An article adjacent to the above cited story presented a lone automotive success story. According to a recent Wall Street Journal, "Volkswagen AG posted solid earnings and stuck to its full-year outlook and said it expects to boost its market share next year." The article states that Volkswagen is the only major European auto maker that has not issued a profit warning.

As marketers we have to ask why; why is one company posting gains while others are in decline? Let's, as consumers, analyze Volkswagen. Volkswagen did not base its profitability on trucks and SUV's. But that's only a partial explanation and relates more to profits than growth in market share. For a more complete answer we have to analyze Volkswagen's marketing, both in the U.S. and internationally.

1. The *WSJ* article attributes much of their success to developing markets in emerging economies, citing China and Brazil.

2. When you think of small, fuel efficient cars, you picture a Japanese or Korean manufactured product. Toyota has been so successful, that most of the manufacturers from Asia design their vehicles to compete with the comparable Toyota model. But for the discerning American youth that want a distinctive vehicle, something different from their grandmother, Volkswagens are their product.

In the U.S., Volkswagen's market strategy has been highly focused on young auto buyers. From the "flower car" bug to sharp, fuel efficient sedans. None of them large, but all of them designed around the priorities of people in their 20's and their young families.

3. Volkswagen's advertising is absolutely distinctive. Mercedes ads can easily be confused with BMW; Ford, GM and Chrysler ads are so similar it seems they must share the same ad agency. But no one confuses a VW ad. A 1950's era black "bug" hosting a talk show format with a music section and the car interviews celebrities. To introduce their mini-van, a female spokesperson begs female viewers not to become pregnant simply for the joy of German engineering as found in the new VW.

Now, let's apply this to the funeral business; particularly the funeral business in your community. Take a moment to consider your place in the market and your competitors. Most communities have a funeral home that depends too much on profits from traditional funerals and operates with too much overhead, just like GM's dependence on trucks. They consider themselves the very best firm in town because their cremation rate is so low, but that's simply a reflection of their flawed marketing and advertising.

Then there's the Ford; not as many funerals as GM, even with lower prices. Open the newspaper to the obituary page and take a look at the ads *(if there are any; newspaper rates have reached such a high level, fewer funeral homes can justify newspaper advertising)*. Every ad in the paper looks the same; the names of the advertisers can be transferred to any of the other ads and would be just as applicable.

Increasingly, there are a number of cremation services and discounters; we'll refer to them as the Asian manufacturers because they all look alike.

But where is the Volkswagen? The company that designs an image around that segment of the market everyone else considers undesirable or too small to focus on. Families that want cremation, but don't trust the discounter to provide the service and quality *(peace of mind)* they want when selecting cremation.

There was a time not long ago that simply offering cremation made a funeral home different; the consumer is learning that every funeral home offers some form of cremation service. But to what extent do funeral homes take the additional step of explaining the options families have when they select cremation? How many funeral arrangers still assume families preferring cremation only want the minimal?

Do yourself a favor; pull out all of your arrangements over the past six months and plot each arranger's average sale as it applies to cremation. Very likely the averages will be widely disparate; some arrangers do ok when meeting with cremation families, but some are abysmal. *Whose fault is this?* Not the arranger; he's doing the best he can with what he has to work with.

The fault is management's; Volkswagen's success is not because the dealers are superior, but because Volkswagen marketing positioned the product in the consumer's mind to create demand. Certainly the local dealer maintained a consistent advertising message and trained sales people to interact effectively; but it all started with a marketing strategy to pursue what American car companies considered an undesirable segment of the market. A market that is too small to pursue because the Japanese had it locked up. Volkswagen saw the same market and made it a target.

10 Marketing Lessons from the American Auto Industry

No two industries are exactly the same; particularly a service-based, family ownership-dominated profession like funeral service, and a manufacturing industry with large barriers to entry like the auto industry. But all industries are similar in terms of managing their image and responding to the consumer, and in this regard the American auto industry allows us the luxury of examining our own shortcomings at their expense.

American automobile companies have come a long way in improving their product quality, but changing brand loyalty has proven to be a greater challenge than building better cars. A current Ford Motor advertising campaign solicits demographically targeted drivers to test drive a Ford vehicle ostensibly as part of a market research project. The objective is to overcome car owners' inclination to purchase the same brand vehicle purchased in the past. The campaign's objective is to demonstrate that once an individual tests a Ford Motor product, they prefer it to other brands.

The most common complaint voiced by funeral home operators in new communities or that have invested millions in new or improved facilities is the challenge of shifting volume to their funeral home. Ironically, the same complaint is common among new vendors to funeral industry. Consumers are typically not logical; they often don't bother to compare prices or services, and if they do shop prices they often miss the value quotient altogether. Consumers who state that convenience is their most important criteria won't use the closest funeral home. There is no one silver bullet that will result in increased volume; instead it is a long term process that involves multiple and diverse efforts to reach the consumer in the way that each individual wants to be reached.

1. The greatest challenge to the image of American cars is the fact Detroit auto makers depend too much on price incentives and rebates. A product's image is tarnished when pricing incentives become too common. Lexus, Mercedes, BMW, Audi, Volvo, Range Rover, Cadillac and other quality auto lines seldom, if ever, offer price reductions. Instead they promote "Certified Used Cars" as a better value than a new American car, which overcomes the price argument while at the same time strengthening the quality message.

This is exactly the challenge the cemetery industry faces but refuses to address. Offering free veterans' spaces, then attempting to up-sell, has caused many consumers to question the value of ground burial. What's interesting is that all of the American auto companies have the same challenge; Chrysler's sale to Mercedes, and the incorporation of Mercedes parts and manufacturing standards were not sufficient to change the consumers' attitudes about Chrysler's products.

Similarly, cemeteries that have not offered free spaces or used other bait and switch tactics, have been tarnished by the price-based advertising of their competitors. Even historic cemeteries with hundreds of private mausoleums bearing the names of historic American families are experiencing difficulties selling grave sites. The cemetery industry will suffer as a whole until the industry realizes their challenge is not a matter of price, but a matter of convincing consumers they actually want to be memorialized in a cemetery.

2. General Motors Chairman and CEO, Rick Wagoner (a recent speaker at a Preferred Funeral Directors International conference held in Detroit) is quoted by the WSJ as saying, *"Building a better car and assuming people will buy it doesn't work; GM can do a better job marketing its vehicles."*

Typically the difference between the top three funeral homes in a market is not a matter of better service, better facilities, better cars or even better people. Instead it is a matter of superior marketing. Today's leading funeral homes are the ones that stepped up their marketing ahead of the competition. Advertising budgets at leading funeral homes nationally continue to swell beyond the minimum 3.5% recommended by many consultants to as much as 8%, 9%, and 10% of gross sales (which includes at-need and pre-need sales).

3. As the American auto companies improve their products to catch up with the Japanese, the competition is also improving, thus setting new, higher-quality standards. A funeral home that is attempting to catch a competitor by employing the advertising tactics the leader implemented ten years ago will find themselves behind in other areas. Along with advertising and public relations, arrangement room strategies are where today's leading funeral homes are focusing their attention. Merchandising is as important a marketing function as is media-based advertising.

One of the challenges facing the American auto companies is the "wheeler/dealer" perception of domestic car dealerships. The import car companies have convinced younger car buyers in general, and women in particular, that they will be treated more fairly and with greater respect at their dealerships than at Ford, GM and Chrysler; and in some respects this is true *(something you know if you have ever owned a Lexus).* Saturn, GM's answer to popular foreign cars, has a "no haggle" pricing policy at all of its dealerships. Notice how many young people hold Saturn in high regard; is the car that much better than other GM products or is it the dealership environment they appreciate?

How often have you heard funeral directors compared to "used car salesmen," particularly when the subject turns to caskets and burial vaults? In many communities, particularly high cremation markets, funeral directors are perceived at the same level as aggressive sales people and the U.S. Congress. Is this because funeral directors try too hard to sell quality caskets? Sometimes, but not often; instead funeral arrangers are held in low regard because they do not possess the skills and tools necessary to perform their job in a manner the consumer expects; professionals are expected to be refined in their presentation. Way too often, funeral directors place the emphasis on getting an arrangement completed within a set time period as opposed to focusing on the process.

4. Many funeral home owners wonder why families won't select their funeral home, even when they have lower prices or superior facilities, or both. Again, the challenge is very similar to the auto companies. Although a family may own a particular brand automobile, they experience other brand vehicles owned by friends or rent vehicles from other manufacturers when traveling. Similarly, families that prefer a funeral home will visit others for visitations and funerals. Controlling what happens during these exposures contributes to future business.

Often, the model vehicles available at Hertz and other rental companies are the products that can't compete successfully against others on the dealership floors, so the manufacturers sell them in bulk to the car rental companies. As such, the consumers' experience with the American-made vehicle may very well be negative simply because they are renting one of the company's least successful models.

Many funeral home owners use the argument that their families are not requesting video tributes, on-site crematories, reception rooms, children rooms, etc. as reasons for not incorporating innovative ideas. When families visit the facility they notice the absence of features and services they have experienced elsewhere. Unlike most businesses, funeral homes have an inherent opportunity to display their products and services; but too often the products we put on display do not represent our best.

5. For most of the past two decades, American auto companies focused their attention on high profit trucks and SUV's where there was less competition from imports and higher profits. Unfortunately, these vehicles consume more fuel, and demand has dropped precipitously with rising oil prices. Today's auto sales are focusing on the four door sedans, a relatively low-profit vehicle that Detroit ignored for many years. Foreign manufacturers own this segment of the market with 54% of car buyers loyal to imports according to JD Powers, an auto industry research group. In an effort to compete with these strong brands, GM has placed Toyotas and Hondas in Chevy and Saturn dealerships so customers could test drive the competition to compare.

The cremation rate has been increasing for the past twenty years, achieving levels of 70% and even 80% in some markets. Even in traditional markets, funeral homes will have 15% and 20% cremation. Instead of changing to meet the demands of the cremation consumer during this period, funeral homes focused on the higher profit traditional business leaving cremation families to minimal cremation services and cremation societies. As such, many consumers assume cremation means no funeral, no memorial and no cemetery, and that cremation should not cost more than $1000.

Overcoming this mindset involves advertising cremation and training staff members to be responsive to cremation families. Realize that cremation families are simply ignorant and need to be educated, which is the obligation of funeral homes and cemeteries.

6. Detroit's auto makers suffer from too many dealerships. Toyota, now the largest auto producing company in the world, has only 1400 dealerships in the U.S., compared to GM's 7,000, Ford's 4800 and Chrysler supporting 3600. In comparison, there are only 500 Mercedes dealerships in the U.S., and only 300 Lexus dealers. There is an indirect correlation between auto company profitability and the number of dealerships; the more dealerships a company has, the lower the manufacturer's profits.

Small auto dealers capture just enough sales to meet their overhead, and they stubbornly stay in business, even when the property value greatly exceeds the value of their business. These companies do not advertise at a level necessary to compete, instead they drain sales from larger dealerships based upon personal relationships. Ironically, the small dealers are actually less price competitive than the larger dealers.

In 1979, the average funeral home served approximately 100 cases annually, which represented a very good family business given the fact that 95% of the calls were full funerals. With a declining death rate, of which only 70% involve burial, and many of them are going to discounters, the demand for traditional funeral service is in decline. In 1979, there were approximately 22,000 funeral homes, today there are about 25,000; a disproportionate number of which are located in large, northeastern cities and states that are experiencing significant population declines, particularly among seniors that retire elsewhere.

Many small funeral businesses survive based upon personal relationships, although their services lack the personalization features popular with consumers. The smaller firms, desperate to remain open, are often the subject of local newspaper reports of embezzling pre-need funds and failing to provide FTC required price lists. Many of the firms embroiled in the unfolding body parts scandals are very low-volume firms located in the northeast that got involved in this scheme to create additional cash flow. As such, there is a price to be paid by the profession for these struggling companies.

The American auto makers would like very much to buy out or close down thousands of dealerships, but cannot due to franchise agreements created many years ago, and state franchise laws designed to protect small businesses. In other words, archaic laws created to serve a narrow purpose during another era are undermining American businesses' ability to compete, just as archaic state licensure laws protect unproductive, marginal funeral businesses. All of the positive promotional efforts undertaken by larger, family-owned funeral businesses are negated by the unethical, and sometimes illegal activities of struggling businesses protected by their funeral licenses.

7. The American auto companies, in contrast to foreign manufacturers, have a tendency to introduce new model names every several years as opposed to maintaining model designators over a long period of time. In contrast, BMW and Mercedes have used the same simple model designators for generations; Toyota introduced the Camry and Corolla when the company began sending vehicles to this country in the 1970's. One of Ford Chief Executive Officer Alan Mulally's initiatives is to retain the model names consumers are familiar with as a means of building loyalty. Further, he wants to bring back advertising slogans, such as *"Have you driven a Ford lately?"*

Most advertising companies will encourage clients to change logos and to coin new slogans to create advertising work. The reality is the fundamental issues in funeral service from the consumers' perspective have not changed. Consumers have reiterated core issues in market research studies over the past 25 years (not necessarily in this order):

- Reputation
- Convenience
- Flexibility in services
- Flexibility in pricing

Advertising messages echoing these issues build brand image over a long period of time. This is not to say funeral homes should run the same advertisement for years at a time; the productivity of any advertisement will diminish with use. However, the fundamental messages in these advertisements should not change.

8. Because of product loyalty, much of the American companies' efforts to compete with imports fail simply because the consumer's attitudes against American products are so deeply ingrained. Even with advances in quality, design and value, 60% of trade-ins for new Chevrolets are other GM vehicles. As such, the dealership's efforts to compete with the imports fail simply because the target audience is never exposed to the message. It is for this reason GM abandoned the idea of having competitors' cars on their lots for comparison test drives.

9. Ford's most profitable car model is the Crown Victoria, which is very popular with seniors. The technology on this model has not changed over the past fifteen years, meaning it is basically the same vehicle, which holds re-tooling costs to a minimum resulting in high profits on each car sold. While it is great that Ford has locked into a profitable demographic, they did so at the expense of future sales as the company cannot shake the reputation of manufacturing stodgy, large cars that younger consumers hold in disdain.

Many funeral businesses have not invested in their facilities to make them consistent with contemporary standards. Today's seniors are more accepting of businesses, taking them as they are and tolerating their deficiencies. Baby boomers are not so forgiving. Baby boomers' standards are established by the hotels and restaurants they visit. They like well-lit environments, comfortable furniture (as opposed to the infamously uncomfortable Victorian antiques so popular with Northeastern and Midwestern funeral homes).

Baby boomers want the funeral home to provide transportation to and from the funeral home for their surviving, infirmed family members, not too many steps (if any) and handicap restrooms near the visitation rooms. Modern funeral homes have available computers for the families to work on obituaries and video tributes. They expect the crematory and reception rooms to be onsite.

Certainly, these features represent a significant cost in infrastructure, and may seem unnecessary, but the funeral industry is in a period when more and more funeral homes are closing each year, which raises the question, is an investment in your facilities to elevate your competitive position in the market too great a cost, or a necessity? Had Ford and GM made long-term decisions during the 1970's when the Japanese and Germans were upgrading their facilities, their bonds may not be considered junk bonds today.

10. A great deal of funeral home advertising is directed to families that already prefer them. The best example is church bulletin advertising and calendars. Instead of circulating calendars or bulletins to churches where the firm does little or no business, the advertising is directed to churches churches where the funeral home already does the majority of calls as a kind of a "reward." Instead of rewarding the church, these efforts reward the printing companies that receive the payments.

Summary: The economy is sinking into recession (or a deeper recession). People will be losing their jobs, and baby boomers will be looking for ways to maintain their retirement portfolios. It could be a tough environment for a couple years. This is a perfect environment to redefine your business. Convince families that they can save thousands by avoiding cemetery costs, yet have a meaningful, memorable service with cremation. Who knows, maybe the Wall Street Journal will write an article about the funeral business that did things differently.

CHAPTER 22

Change Is in the Air

The American public is primed for change. Our new president ran on a campaign with that theme and the economic crisis is convincing society that we, as a nation, can no longer practice business or our personal lifestyles, as we have in the past.

The greatest challenge in life is breaking one's own pattern to do something new and different. The best example of this is to change your lifestyle enough to actually lose five pounds. If you're a baby boomer you can relate. It's not just exercise, and it's not just diet; even something as seemingly innocuous as a cup of coffee can undermine your weight loss efforts. The point being, whether for a nation or an individual, improvement requires change, and change can be difficult.

Funeral directors have been lambasted for years as being reticent to change; the reality is funeral businesses have been extremely responsive to society's changes. Having visited hundreds of funeral homes annually for several decades, the changes the public witnesses in funeral service is remarkable. Candidly, if the cemetery industry was half as responsive as funeral directors, they wouldn't still be running free veteran spaces advertisements but would be dealing with the real problem of presenting the value a family derives from a cemetery memorial.

Nonetheless, after all the changes funeral directors and funeral businesses have implemented, funeral thinking must continue to change; and one of the areas where we have to change the most is in how marketing budgets are invested. The collapse of the newspaper industry over the past six months is a culmination of over twenty years of steady decline. Even seniors are reading the newspaper less; but seniors' habits are not the issue because the target audience for funeral home advertising is not the 80 year old, or even the 70 year old; it's their baby boomer child; and this group has never subscribed to newspapers.

Another total waste of funeral home marketing budgets is the yellow pages. Just as people no longer get their news from the newspaper, they no longer refer to the telephone directory to select a funeral home. Funeral home selection is far more complicated than that. Funeral home selection is viral; information spreads by word of mouth; particularly something families purchase as seldom as death care. They ask their friends, or they shop around; the consumer is too well educated to simply select a funeral home from a number of ads in the yellow pages.

So the media used to connect with the consumer has changed. Most funeral homes have a Web site, and nearly all larger funeral businesses advertise on some electronic media *(cable or broadcast television, radio).* But for advertising to be successful, the advertiser must do something special. Advertising that promotes an event will be more successful than a generic image ad that any funeral home could run. An example is The Bass Pro Shop's Christmas season campaign. This past Christmas shopping season was dismal for retailers made worse by the fact that every retailer in the country knew in advance it was going to be a challenge, so most cut back in their holiday promotional efforts.

One exception was The Bass Pro Shops. Certainly Christmas shopping represents a big opportunity for The Bass Pro Shops just as it does for every retailer, but maybe not as important to them as it is to most simply because the Christmas shopping season follows deer season which, for a hunting and fishing retailer, is the busiest season of the year. So, The Bass Pro Shops could very well have taken a low profile with Christmas just as most retailers did and wait for the next big hunting/fishing season, but they didn't.

Instead they went all out for Christmas in the tradition of the big New York City department retailers in the past. They had camping expeditions in their parking lots and Christmas wonderlands in their stores. They went all out at a time when their competitors were cutting back. As a result, families came to the stores for the events, and stayed to shop when they otherwise may not have.

Let's apply that mentality to funeral service. A recent survey published by NFDA indicates that the majority of respondents are reacting to the reduced profit margins by cutting back on their promotion, facility improvements and other expenditures. Will there ever be a better time to differentiate yourself from the competition? During a period when your competition will be less visible than in the past and their facility will be looking more tired and used, you have an excellent opportunity to stand out. An investment in new and different marketing efforts will be more productive in 2009 and beyond than it has in the past decade or possibly the decade to follow.

Now, let's take this discussion a step further; is advertising even the best use of your marketing investment? For any advertising effort to be successful it must be continuous. Television or radio advertisements must run at least thirty plus weeks per year, newsletters should be quarterly, and your Web site needs search engine software to get the top listings when a consumer searches for information online. All of this costs; in reality a productive media budget for most funeral businesses, even in small towns, should be in the $40,000 range.

When advertising is successful; when it really hits a home run, does it generate a funeral? Not really; it generates a phone call. Whether calling for information or prices, advertising succeeds when it causes a consumer to make an inquiry. And the reality is, for most funeral homes, particularly those in the 300 calls or smaller range, this is when many funeral businesses lose the opportunity to serve a family. Funeral home staff is painfully unprepared to respond professionally, knowledgeably and persuasively to an inquiry phone call. They simply don't know how because they have never been trained.

Let's just start with the way the telephone is initially answered:

- "Hello" with no indication that the caller has reached a business.
- "Funeral Home" with no indication as to which business they have contacted.
- "Gould's" the name of the firm, but no reference to funeral home, mortuary, etc.

And this isn't the greatest fault; there does not seem to be any sense of importance placed on inquiry phone calls. If the call is not a "death call," staff acts as if it just doesn't matter.

Ask yourself how much it would mean to your business if staff knew how to respond to a telephone inquiry? How much more business would I receive from a $2000 investment in telephone training versus several weeks of advertising?

Of course training does not end with the telephone. Just as funeral home staff is inadequate at handling inquiries, the entire funeral home environment is counterproductive to making productive cremation arrangements. Arrangement rooms are stuck in small, out of the way rooms with poor lighting and inadequate electronics. Arrangers continue to focus on the state-required mortality form as opposed to the family's priorities. Even the fact that funeral directors prefer payment with a credit card versus an insurance policy assignment demonstrates how little thought management has invested in determining how best to manage the arrangement process.

The interest charges accumulate each month the family takes to pay off a funeral bill on their credit card at 1.5% to 2% per month. What impact does that have on the family when they see that recurring expense on their credit card statement? Isn't it likely that they begin to question the value of a funeral when it takes them months and months to pay for it? An insurance assignment costs a flat 5% or less regardless of how long it takes the assignment company to collect from the insurance company. Even if they must go to court to collect, the family only pays the assignment fee. According to Dan Goldman at Jackman Financial, "Funeral directors would be providing families a wonderful service if they would only explain to them why they should apply for an insurance assignment versus charging the funeral bill."

Instead of leaving the family with a negative reminder of the funeral cost, why not deliver a positive product that will serve the family well and reinforce the value received from the funeral home. An executor is assigned the responsibility of settling the deceased's estate whenever there is a death. The executor is first flattered that the family trusted them with this responsibility but soon comes to realize the incredible responsibility that has been placed on them. It's not easy and it takes time. It takes on average 6 – 18 months to settle an estate, therefore the funeral home is providing consistent value for that period of time – much longer than most traditional aftercare programs.

A lawyer typically charges $100+ to draft and send a single estate-related letter. Families report savings of $500 - $1000+ using the template letters in the kit. The Executor's Toolkit is a wonderful product that funeral homes have been presenting to families for nearly a decade. Researched by attorneys, the Toolkit educates executors and guides them through the process. Funeral homes invest thousands and thousands annually to provide aftercare services that consumers, for the most part, perceive of little value when something as inexpensive as the Executor's Toolkit would be of so much greater value.

Summary: For decades many funeral directors, particularly at mid-size and smaller independent funeral homes have argued that changing their modus operandi somehow translated into a lower level of service to the family. Who are we trying to fool? Reluctance to change is simply a lazy-minded approach to doing one's job. If you want to serve families while improving your business, it will only come from change. Start today.

CHAPTER 23

Finding Business Success by Doing Things Differently

What if the fundamentals of running a successful funeral business were counterintuitive to all of your practical experience? All of the experience your family accumulated over generations running funeral homes was diametrically opposite what you should be doing to make a profit in this business. It has happened in other, much simpler industries than funeral and cemetery businesses. Leadership in the luggage industry has shifted from well-established companies like Hartmann, Samsonite and Hillenbrand's former American Tourister division, to Tumi and Versace. Profitability in the airline industry has shifted from legacy carriers, to Southwest and Jet Blue. The Japanese taught American auto companies how to make a profit from small cars, and now Hyundai and Kia are teaching the Japanese. Department stores of the 50's, 60's and 70's have been replaced by big box retailers, and much more profitable specialty retailers. Three big broadcast companies have surrendered profitability to premium cable networks.

All of these industries are victims of social and technological change. Industries, with firm foundations in society trying to keep up with society as technology creates opportunities for new concepts that fit better with contemporary lifestyles.

Compared to most industries in the U.S., the funeral and cemetery industries are very old. In addition to being old, neither has changed a great deal over the past 100 years in terms of technology, ownership, or operating practices. It should be expected that there would be fundamental philosophies or axioms that are generally accepted by practitioners that actually hinder progress, even restrict profitability and success.

For example, funeral home owners can not overcome the idea that volume, any volume, is good for business. This assumption is fundamentally wrong and contributes to the financial challenge of thousands of funeral homes nationally. Other misconceptions are that the consuming public perceives some value in embalming and caskets. Families see value in memories; they have funerals for the benefit of gathering friends and family members, sharing and making memories. Profitability will come when funeral directors begin to merchandise services and memories as they merchandise caskets and suits today.

The challenge on the cemetery side is even more compelling. Funeral directors are moving in the right direction, but cemetery owners have made no apparent gains against their greatest challenge, which also represents their greatest opportunity.

Research conducted nationally indicates 83% of middle income families that want cemetery space already own it; and 90% of affluent consumers wanting cemetery property (or a mausoleum) already own it. Any research data can be somewhat flawed, and certainly it will vary from one locale to another. But even if this data is 80% accurate, it defines the challenge cemetery salespeople are having selling cemetery space. Pre-need cemetery sales over 50 years have filled the pipeline and the growing preference for cremation is limiting future demand. Deal with it: the majority of people who want cemetery property already own it, and the others don't want it. Once the industry accepts this simple reality they will create the opportunity for their future success.

Cremation families don't believe cemeteries have products for them. Funeral homes lost cremation families to minimum service cremation providers (i.e., cremation societies) until they began advertising cremation services. Today, families receive cremated remains from funeral homes and crematories, take them home for scattering, or let them sit in the back of closets for years. Funeral homes nationally hold thousands of cremated remains just waiting for family members to retrieve them. Every family is a prospect for cemetery products, but without fundamental education, these families will continue to treat cremated remains as unwanted waste from an industrial process.

The cremation consumer considers themselves rugged individualists; protecting the environment by rejecting culture and tradition, rejecting what they perceive to be the high cost of dying, and fearing that family members will never visit their grave. The reality is they are ignorant. They don't know what's available and it's not their fault. It's the death care industry's fault, funeral, cemetery and vendors, for not running fundamental advertising to explain how death care is relevant.

The cemetery industry has consistently rejected all forms of advertising other than lead generating direct mail and telephone solicitation. Direct mail response rates have declined from 20 to 30 per cent from when it began following World War II to .2% today while postage and handling costs have increased several hundred per cent and telemarketing has been rendered obsolete by answering machines and the "no call list." Yet the industry continues to dump mail and flirt with huge fines in an effort to sell traditional burial. Wake up – society has moved on and so should the cemetery industry.

The challenge for the cemetery industry is to grow the market for cremation products with information. The present demand for these products is minimal, but the potential is huge. Exploiting the opportunity is a matter of accepting the challenge to recognize the change in society and to become a part of the new traditions. There is some urgency in this matter as ultimately, the consumer will find an answer to their dilemma. Already churches, universities, country clubs and other businesses are installing columbarium niches on their properties. Consumers relate to these locales, and find the option appealing. Consumers prefer the serenity of a cemetery, so the industry is in a superior position to compete. It is only a potentially better hand; there is no reason to believe consumers will seek out the cemetery; the cemetery must create the demand.

For nearly two hundred years, funeral service had a firm foundation in American culture based upon Judeo/ Christian priorities. Even after the American culture shifted away from church attendance, consumers purchased funerals because they were a little embarrassed to admit their deceased loved was un-churched. Instead of the clergy attending the funeral as a friend with a few words of salvation, they received honorariums to say nice things about people they didn't know. After a few decades some people came to conclude it was more embarrassing to be identified with the church than not, so they stopped having funerals.

What if funeral industry leaders had rethought their business formulas before they were on the verge of bankruptcy? What if they had challenged everything they knew to be true about their businesses and looked at it from a different point of view? A popular business book, "Blue Ocean Strategy" challenges us to do just that. The book's premise is that every industry operates upon generally accepted priorities that lead them to compete in oceans turned red from bloody competition. While other companies in the same industries restructure their businesses to meet consumers' priorities and to thrive in highly profitable, temporary legal monopolies while other companies race to keep up.

At one time, all motels had restaurants and bars simply because inns had traditionally offered food and lounges. Over time, food service became a drag on profitability, and motels started to spring up on exits across the country that provided a superior room at a very competitive price; and they did very well until the legacy names caught up.

How different would the funeral business be if it was structured around consumer priorities versus what we have always believed funeral homes should be? What do we learn about ourselves when we objectively study the industry?

- We believe funeral homes should be large and auspicious.
- Arrangers must be licensed by the state to embalm, even though the best arrangers may never work in an embalming room.
- Funeral homes should be inconveniently located downtown as opposed to where people live.
- Funeral homes should be dependent upon burial to realize a profit.
- Caskets should be displayed like automobiles in selection rooms.
- Funeral homes should derive more profit from selling merchandise instead of their facilities and staff.
- Success in business is dependent upon providing superior service even though the consumer can't tell the difference between good service and poor service.

What does the consumer really want, and how could operators achieve superior profits by breaking with the past?

- It is becoming increasingly obvious consumers put a higher priority on convenience than large facilities.
- Successful funeral homes don't necessarily give superior service, and consumers wouldn't recognize good service if they did. Instead, families select funeral homes based upon personal relationships, convenience and a perception of value and price.
- Instead of caskets, people want memories. Focus groups commissioned by four different vendor companies in diverse regions of the country all drew the same conclusion – there is far more profit in creating memories and keepsakes than in caskets.
- Instead of visitations, families want receptions with food service.
- Instead of graveside services, many families want memorial services.
- Instead of seeking moderate profits from families preferring ground burial and mausoleums, funeral homes should learn to generate superior profits from cremation memorialization and personalization.

CHAPTER 24

Prospering from Social Trends

Trends in funeral service result from megatrends in society. Traditional funeral services reflected the nation's abiding religious faith. Pre-need was created to allow lower income families to afford traditional funerals during a period when the working class aspired to middle class values. The trend toward cremation without services came about as families became less churched and decentralized as the nation became more mobile. Through all of this transition, funeral directors have questioned consumers' motivations and pondered what can be done to return the industry to past levels of relevance and profitability. Of course the answers are not in the past; instead prosperity and profit comes from connecting death care businesses with megatrends moving forward.

Presently society's communal attention is fixed on the economy and the economy will impact families' decision making for months, even years to come. In some ways the declining economy could have positive impact on the death care businesses. For example:

- For the past fifty years, seniors have been retiring far away from their long-term homes and communities, particularly those that lived in colder, industrial states with higher taxes and higher costs of living. This migration was fueled by escalating property values in these regions and lower costs of living in southern states. The declining economy will interrupt this megatrend as seniors will encounter difficulty selling their homes at any price, and the cost of living in Florida and other southern states has increased to a level of parity or even greater than the cost of living in the north.

  The declining economy has altered the retirement plans of millions of baby boomers. The bailout packages have incurred massive federal debt which will further challenge the already questionable Social Security funds. Baby boomers will continue to work from economic necessity.

Society's increasing costs will challenge the prevailing attitudes toward healthcare. It is estimated that 80% of all the health costs incurred by an American are incurred during their last eighteen months of life. How long can this expensive proclivity continue in an economy that creates less and less? Declining levels of health care will keep families closer together and shorten life spans.

All of these factors will keep people in their homes, which will increase the number of deaths in the northern states. When these seniors die in their hometowns, their families will be more likely to have funeral services versus the minimum cremation they would have had in retirement communities. This should positively impact cemetery sales, as well as funeral home sales.

- The declining economy has focused attention on the value of manufacturing jobs as the American auto companies are subsidized by the government to keep people working in auto plants, as well as auto dealerships nationally. The entire citizenry is getting an economic lesson as we the people become stock holders in American industry. With an appreciation for the economic impact of American manufacturing, it is likely some consumers will prefer American-made caskets. Certainly, funeral homes that offer Chinese caskets could argue that lower-cost Chinese caskets are healthy for the funeral business, but healthy and strong American casket companies make huge contributions to the funeral businesses in ways offshore manufacturers do not. In many ways, a healthy death care vendor community contributes to a healthy funeral profession.

- The declining economy will keep funeral directors in their jobs as people seek stability. This should lower operating costs at funeral businesses and contribute to greater productivity as experienced people make fewer errors and require less supervision.

- Poor economies typically generate higher caliber employment candidates for professions that have difficulty recruiting during periods of economic expansion. Police and fire departments, teachers, and other professions have always benefited from recessions, as have cemeteries, as the caliber of salespeople improves. Mortuary schools should expect more and better qualified applicants which will elevate the quality of their graduates.

Just as funeral businesses can benefit in the short term from the challenging economy, they can also benefit from emerging megatrends in society. The economic downturn, regardless of severity, is temporary. At some point, housing will regain value, people will eventually retire, and the employment picture will improve. But there are megatrends evolving that will a have long-term impact on the American landscape just as the diminishing importance of religion and mobility have had. The most significant megatrend may be the growing sensitivity to the environment.

The green movement is visible in all facets of American society; the earliest signs were the development of green zones such as local and national parks. Then recycling became a national effort, followed by natural and organic foods and fuel-efficient transportation, followed by environmental home and workplace construction with more efficient heating and cooling systems. The green movement will permanently change lifestyles over time.

Joe Sehee has appeared at hundreds of association meetings over the past several years as an evangelist for the green movement in death care. His primary message is that the death care industry has an opportunity to embrace green funerals and natural burial, but if we don't, consumers will find other businesses that will and traditional death care businesses will find themselves competing with green societies just as they have with cremation societies for the past 25 years.

Research studies conducted by MKJ Marketing for funeral homes nationally indicate consumers preferring green funeral services expect to pay more for the environmentally-friendly services than for traditional services, and certainly more than they pay for cremation services. After all, what is environmental about burning fossil fuels versus digging a hole in the ground and burying a biodegradable wooden box containing a body embalmed with fluids that do not contain formaldehyde?

Environmentally-sensitive consumers expect to pay more for green and natural products than they do for traditional products. The federal government subsidized hybrid vehicles (available primarily through Japanese auto companies) to help them launch their more expensive products in the U.S. Whole food stores charge anywhere from 50% to 300% more than main line grocers do for comparable products. Commercial office space lease rates in green buildings average 30% more than office space in traditionally heated and cooled buildings.

Service businesses need innovation. When a concept or product is new and rare, the provider of that service will realize exceptional profits. A good example is the Frank E. Campbell Funeral Home in New York City. As the first modern funeral home built in the early 1900's, the firm attracted the most wealth and prestigious New York families. Even today, a century later, Frank E. Campbell still has $100,000 funerals for the Kennedys and other leading families. By redefining the funeral business, Frank E. Campbell elevated the profession and the value families placed on funeral services.

As more funeral homes were built, the business became more competitive, causing prices to decline in recent years. At some point in the pricing cycle, competition will begin to thin as some providers close their doors. When competition thins, prices should increase. More funeral businesses are closing during this current recession than ever before, but prices have not increased because the death rate remains low. A funeral business introducing a new service, such as reception rooms, an on-site crematory, or green funerals, can charge a premium because the competitors do not offer a competitive service. So, life cycle pricing encourages innovation and investment in established businesses as a means of securing superior profits. In many ways, the green movement might represent the best long-term opportunity in funeral service since Frank E. Campbell built the first modern funeral home in New York City.

American casket companies are already developing green products, embalming fluid companies have formaldehyde-free fluids, and cemeteries are beginning to develop areas for natural burial; so a foundation is being created. But as always has been the case in death care, the greatest obstacles to business success will not be tangible factors like products, but changing the attitudes of the people that work within the profession. Resistance to the green movement already exists; inexplicably many embalmers will argue their preference for formaldehyde-based embalming fluids even knowing the product is a carcinogen.

Embracing the green movement will demand an attitude of acceptance and flexibility that will challenge many licensed practitioners and funeral business owners. Understanding the attributes and limitations of natural products falls under the heading of maintaining currency with changes in the industry; an obligation of any individual that considers themselves a professional.

The green consumer is skeptical, as well as discerning. First, they are affluent which jaundices their perspective on all factors. Traditional funeral service declines began when we lost the support of thought leaders. As celebrities, civic leaders and other visible personalities began to prefer cremation, the middle class began to question the value of expensive funerals. It will take a concerted effort to get the affluent consumer to pay attention to funeral home offerings again. According to Joe Sehee, "The green consumer has disdain for traditional death care offerings and the way they have been approached by these businesses in the past." The traditional cemetery salesperson will have little success with the green consumer if he employs traditional sales tactics; suffice it to say, the cynical consumer will not respond well to photos of ambulances in the night or the question, ***"What will your family be doing tomorrow if you die today"***.

The true green consumer will want to understand how the green funeral or natural burial differs from the traditional services and they will challenge any compromise. Certainly, there are shades of green in that not all cemeteries will be able to offer a completely natural burial immediately. Laws in some states will necessitate some compromises, but anyone presenting green services must be informed and intelligent on the subject to be successful relating to the affluent consumer.

Even advertising green services will require sensitivity on the part of the advertiser. Newspapers are not considered environmentally friendly as newspaper type takes generations to decompose, and few consumers approve of direct mail. Reaching the green consumer will take tact and a level of acumen at manipulating public relations opportunities.

CHAPTER 25

The Task at Hand

Ultimately, all discounters come to an end. The nature of discounting is such that at some point in the businesses' evolution, it is no longer possible or logical to continue business as usual. That's not to say they will necessarily go out of business; some do, others develop a more profitable business plan.

Surviving as a discounter, for an extended period, is difficult. First, there must be a high volume of demand for whatever service or product the discounter is selling. The most successful discounters are in retail household items and clothing simply because there are a lot of willing buyers for everyday items at a below retail price.

Equally important as demand, is a successful strategy for procurement. Most successful discounters have a strategy for reducing the cost of doing business to a level that allows for a profit. Walmart replaced K-Mart as the world's largest retailer, and ultimately forced them into bankruptcy, not because of lower prices at the register, but because Walmart could purchase merchandise at a better price. No other discount retail group can match Walmart in terms of buying.

Target competes successfully through better merchandising. By having trendy items available in season, Target is able to charge enough of a premium for their merchandise to make them profitable, while still staying under the full retail prices department stores charge.

The most precarious discount businesses are those competitors can easily match in price. The discount law firm of Jacoby and Myer grew quickly until other attorneys learned the secret to their success: retail-type advertising, no fee for the initial visit, and representing only those personal injury suits that have a high likelihood of winning.

Another fate for discounters is to simply increase their prices. Some of the death care companies that operate as discounters today were companies that wanted to acquire funeral homes in the 1990's but couldn't because of the high prices the large corporations were paying. Acquisition became so expensive it was a better business plan to open a new facility offering lower prices.

Discounters would prefer less volume and to make more money by operating full-priced, traditional funeral homes. After they accumulate a sufficient level of sales and patronage, they will and have raised their prices. Certainly, price increases will cost them some business but not enough to offset the profits gained by charging more. Once a company has established itself as a low price leader, it can take competitors to convince the public otherwise. As such, funeral homes with a low-cost reputation can maintain that reputation for years after raising their prices.

If all discounters ultimately come to an end, what is the fate of funeral service discounters? This is a critical question:

1. Will they be put out of business by full-service funeral homes reducing their prices?
2. Will the discounters ultimately increase their prices and become full-service funeral homes generating superior sales and revenues?
3. Will traditional funeral homes discover a better way to do business that allows them to serve both the price-sensitive customer and the full-service customer?

If traditional funeral homes are forced to lower their prices in order to remain in business against successful discounters, hundreds, even thousands of funeral homes will be closed. The same will likely happen if funeral service discounters survive long enough to increase their prices to a competitive level. Either way, families that previously went to a traditional funeral home will shift their business to what they believe to be a lower-priced alternative.

The only scenario that maintains the funeral profession as we know it is for traditional funeral homes to effectively compete on a price basis with discounters, while at the same time offering families service options that cause them to buy quality services and merchandise. Accomplishing this necessitates the following:

1. Offer price packages that allow the traditional funeral home to compete on a price level without becoming a discounter.
2. Learn to handle price shoppers effectively.

3. Educate the consumer as to the breadth of services a full-service funeral home firm provides in terms of value.

4. Arrange services the consumer considers outstanding and values even when charged a premium price.

5. Win back the business of affluent consumers.

The most critical challenge for the long-term viability of the death care industry in the U.S., is to win back the business of affluent consumers. For forty years, death care has endeavored to market traditional funerals to mid-income and blue-collar families. In the process, we have lost or are losing the affluent consumer. It's increasingly common to hear professionals and affluent consumers declare how a traditional funeral is right for their parents, but not for them.

Losing the affluent consumer means much more than just an increasing cremation rate and reduced revenues on a few funerals a year. It also means the loss of thought leaders.

Social behavior is influenced by a continuum of fads and trends. Trendsetters initiate fads and trends, a small percentage of the total population that introduces new ideas through their own behavior. The behavior is observed, copied and modified by a larger group that intentionally seeks out alternative behavior as a means of being different. Over time, a sufficient population observes and copies the trendsetters and the behavior becomes a fad. If the fad endures, it becomes a trend.

The original founders and members of cremation societies in the early 19th century sought an alternative to traditional funerals. Like the Hemlock Society members, cremation society members represented a very small segment of the population. So small in fact, implementing their wishes for cremation necessitated joining a society. Funeral traditions change slowly; as such, some 150 years later the national cremation rate is approaching 30%. Nonetheless, a very small group initiated the trend toward simpler services and cremation when a horse-drawn carriage was the common mode of personal transportation.

Blue-collar families represent the primary consumer of traditional funerals today because the affluent consumers of the 1950's, 60's, and early 70's established the standard years ago. But research indicates the influence of those past decades is waning. Increasingly, blue-collar families are beginning to question funeral costs; and when they do, they'll note how a local judge, attorney or doctor recently died and their family "didn't even have a funeral." The strongest endorsement a funeral home can get is the obituary of a respected individual with visiting hours and funeral services.

Winning Back the Affluent Consumer

Successfully marketing to the affluent consumer is different from marketing to the rest of society. Most families feel comfortable knowing they have the same lifestyle as the people they relate to. If the neighbor has a new car, maybe they should be thinking about one. That's why auto salespeople ask you to give their card to your neighbors. Many middle-class widows tell the funeral director, "We want to do the right thing, like everyone else."

Affluent consumers don't want what everyone else wants. Wealthy consumers take pride in being able to afford services and products others cannot. What's the point of being affluent if it doesn't allow you to buy things others can't? "Buy one, get one free" does not motivate a wealthy consumer to buy cemetery property. In fact, it diminishes the value of ground burial and causes them to consider cremation.

The affluent consumer "wants what they want," and they are willing to pay for what they want. Affluent consumers seldom reject a product or service based upon price alone; they are more likely to reject a product based upon value. Affluent consumers will patronize a minimal cremation service but won't patronize a discount funeral home. It's not the funeral cost they reject; they don't want a funeral at any price. Often they will contract with a minimal cremation company for disposition of the body, and have an expensive reception at their country club, yacht club, or clubhouse of their retirement community.

So, what is it the affluent consumer wants? To answer that question we have to study their lifestyle. What businesses do affluent consumers patronize, and how do these businesses treat them? Certainly, affluent consumers visit nice hotels and restaurants. Fortunately, the architecture of contemporary funeral homes resembles these businesses. But there's more to it than that.

Affluent consumers are accustomed to special services that accommodate their needs. Valet parking, concierge service, thoughtful food service, and special accommodations over and above the average. It is in this regard that funeral service is lacking. Funeral homes take great pride in the level of service they provide, but that service extends only as far as the boundaries of the traditional funeral. Affluent consumers do not judge service based upon tradition; they judge service based upon their needs and expectations.

Many services funeral homes could offer are simply too time consuming to be practical. Nonetheless, they are desirable services. Photographing flowers and identifying the giver is time consuming, and may not be important to everyone, but some consumers would pay a premium for the service. It should be offered as an option, just as providing an attendant in the children's room, providing food service following funerals and passed hors d'oeuvres during visitations with live music. They purchase these services when the reception is held at their club.

Research indicates the affluent consumer, particularly those inclined toward cremation, is the most likely to perceive value in personalized funeral services. Video tributes, personalized caskets and vaults, memory boards, and "big mama's kitchen" are innovations on the traditional funeral. The merchandise costs more, and funeral directors charge more for a casket with interchangeable corner pieces. Funeral homes should also charge additional for the other forms of personalization. Personalized funerals require more professional time to arrange, and more labor hours to accomplish. If we don't begin charging for these services now, it will be nearly impossible to do so later. Furthermore, these services need promotional support to be successful. The additional income generated from these services should be reinvested in tools arrangers would use in presenting options.

> *Summary: By aggressively pursuing the blue-collar consumer, death care has sacrificed the business of those consumers most capable of purchasing our best products. Reversing the trend is a matter of repackaging the funeral product in such a way as to offer that consumer willing to pay more, something they perceive of value.*

Over the past 25 years, the greatest challenges to funeral services have come from competitors other than the traditional funeral homes. The greatest challenge today is coming from wedding planners and social clubs, as they endeavor to usurp the service from funeral service. If we don't wholeheartedly accept the concept of event planning, funeral homes will become mortuaries and revenues for the industry could drop as much as 80% as funeral directors become disposition services.

CHAPTER 26

Competing with a Lower Cost Alternative

You're shopping for a new electronic consumer product at an electronics department store. You turn down the aisle with thirty products displayed; you find a group of five with the package of features you want. Price varies little, if any, from one product to the next. One of the options is a brand name you recognize as a quality leader. Which do you select?

All things being equal, consumers will select a leading brand name. The value of a well-established brand name is the inherent confidence consumers have in the name, even when all tangible data suggests there is no difference in products.

What does this have to do with funeral service? The selection of a funeral home has less to do with services, prices, convenience, religion, cremation and pre-need and much more to do with the consumer's perception of the brand name. Just as in retail and other professional services, maintaining a strong brand name will prove the best defense against discount funeral service.

What Is a Brand Name?

Over a period of time, a consumer develops expectations as to how a company will perform. A brand name is the provider's commitment to a customer to meet their expectations, consistently. Satisfying expectations over and over again creates passionate, loyal customers.

Nationally, many funeral homes define the "brand name" concept. Having been part of a community from 50 to 100 + years, residents of a community come to have definite ideas as to what they can expect from the various funeral firms in their community. It can be very difficult to shift appreciable volume from one funeral home to another in communities where the funeral firms have consistently met the consumer's expectations.

On the other hand, if one funeral home disappoints their families by dropping their standards, thus not meeting their consumers' expectations, volume will shift dramatically. It is not at all uncommon for funeral homes to juxtaposition as one generation fails to maintain the standards established by predecessors. This also explains why some acquired firms fail to hold their volume.

Why Is Brand Awareness Important in Funeral Service?

Research indicates 80% of consumers believe all funeral homes are the same, which is to say all brands of VCR's; televisions and other consumer products function similarly. When it is difficult to differentiate between products (i.e., facilities, services, prices, etc.) a funeral home's most important attribute may be the consuming public's perceptions of the firm; in other words, their brand name.

CASE STUDIES:

***#1** A leading southeastern funeral home held approximately 90% market share in a community generating approximately 1400 cases annually. The firm operated facilities in two other communities, neither of which competed successfully against well-established firms in those towns, despite competitive prices, excellent service and facilities. In their home community they held a very strong brand name with tremendous customer loyalty, an advantage non-existent in the other communities. Without the consumer loyalty, a far firm, with far superior resources, was at a competitive disadvantage against lesser firms.*

***#2** When a funeral home has a weak brand name, consumers perceive the firm to be generally inferior. A market research study of four funeral homes in a mid-size, mid-western community found that consumers considered the three leading funeral homes to have very similar image attributes. Each of the three firms had strong name awareness. Respondents to the study had similar ability to recall advertising run by all three of the leading firms.*

In contrast, the fourth funeral home in the study had very low name awareness; in fact only 5% of the respondents could recall seeing any advertising at all from the firm (even though the firm had sponsored a Sunday morning religious program for years).

One of the questions asked about each of the four firms was, "Is it located convenient to where they live?" The three leading firms were perceived much more convenient than the fourth firm, even though all four firms are located within a six-block perimeter.

Many owners lament the diminished loyalty among consumers; it is true, consumer loyalty is not what it once was. The introductions of generic products in department stores, failed promises of quality, and providers' shifting priorities have caused consumers to experiment with new brands. In funeral service, changes in ownership and mobility have eroded the value of some funeral home brand names.

But these changes in consumers' priorities do not devalue the importance of building a strong brand name, just the contrary. It may take a greater commitment over a longer period of time, to build a brand name in today's environment, but the value of the brand is even greater since so few funeral homes have a strong name.

How Is a Strong Brand Name Developed?

There are two strategies for building a strong brand name, the first requires a relatively short amount of time and a huge advertising budget. The second requires a far smaller budget, but a very long time. Both strategies work.

CASE STUDIES:

#3 When America On Line began business, there were two well-established Internet portals. Prodigy and CompuServe had a significant advantage on AOL, as both were funded by large, well-established corporations. Nonetheless, AOL built the strongest brand name, resulting in the most users, through an immense advertising campaign. AOL used every conceivable distribution avenue to put starter floppy discs in the hands of every computer owner in the country. The promotional effort was so comprehensive, many Internet users thought AOL and the Internet were one and the same.

***#4** A Midwest, metro-area funeral home accomplished the same phenomena using extensive television advertising over a ten-year period.*

In 1994, the client commissioned a prospective trade area research study to determine the opportunity for a new funeral home in another section of their city. Although the firm did not have a funeral home within ten miles of the studied area, the research study indicated the client's name awareness was twice as strong as any funeral home serving the studied area at that time. Not only were residents of the studied area familiar with the client, a majority of families living in the area indicated they would select that firm if their facility was not located so far away.

Based upon projected at-need volume for the new funeral home, the client invested significantly in a new building. While the building was under construction, a discount funeral service was founded in the immediate area of the new building. The discount firm has grown to approximately 900 cases annually. Nonetheless, the client's firm has met the projected at-need volume and operates profitably.

The strong advertising campaign (along with the firm's consistently high standards of service) created loyalty for the brand name so strong, it was able to compete successfully with the discount funeral home.

Summary: Ten Reasons to Invest in a Strong Brand Name:

10. Better receivables: newly opened funeral homes, low cost alternatives and weaker firms in a market all have far more trouble with receivables than do the market leaders. For the past decade, cash flow experts have encouraged leading firms to revamp their payment terms. Some have, many have not simply because receivables are not a significant problem for the leading firms.

9. The most often volunteered source for selecting a funeral home is a recommendation from a friend or relative. A strong brand name promotes "word of mouth advertising."

8. Hold and attract quality staff. Turnover among professional staff is always less of a problem with the prestigious firms. If for no other reason, staff members of lesser firms prefer the prestige of working for the leader in their community.

7. A strong brand name affords more strategic options. You can build volume by holding a competitive price or charge premium prices without losing volume.

6. 80% of consumers consider all funeral homes to be the same. A strong brand name may be the only differentiating factor between funeral homes.

5. Reduce risk when attempting to expand trade area. A strong brand name creates demand for services. Demand for new facilities builds faster.

4. Facilitate pre-need sales. Every insurance company and third-party selling company attempts to win the business of the market leader before pursuing the lesser firms in a community, simply because they know their lead generating and sales efforts will be more productive.

3. Younger generations are not as brand loyal; it will take a stronger effort to build their awareness and patronage.

2. Society is mobile. The population within your market is dynamic with people moving in and out constantly. Your future business may be dependent upon the image people moving into the community have of your firm.

1. A strong brand name will be the first line of defense against lower-cost, alternative services.

CHAPTER 27

Why Funeral Arrangers Are So Difficult to Train

Since casket and vault companies began introducing merchandising systems to funeral service in the 1970's, vendors have expressed frustration with funeral directors for not providing families with their product information. Whether it be urn vaults, upgraded register books, funeral jewelry, pre-need insurance products, or any number of ancillary personalization and memorial gifts such as casket blankets, portraits, printed products and heirlooms, staff arrangers have resisted pressure from owners, supervisors, and sometimes even family members, to introduce the features and benefits of products. Why?

The typical rational is that funeral directors don't want to be salespeople as if being a sales professional is to be damned. But you notice many arrangers won't even involve family members in a discussion of what the deceased enjoyed about life or what the deceased meant to them. Instead they insist on focusing their attention on administrative details as if collecting vital statistics will somehow relieve a family's grief.

A more compelling reason could be that arrangers have no incentive to take risks. Look at it from the arrangers' perspective. When a funeral director presents a new concept or product to a family they are risking a rebuke from a family member for putting too much pressure on them, which will certainly result in a poor rating on a customer satisfaction survey followed by a meeting with the owner or manager.

The consumer has minimal expectations from a funeral. They don't expect to be wowed; in fact they mostly just want to get through the process; so the funeral arranger has a very low standard to meet. The family simply expects the funeral director to deliver whatever he/she promises; as a result the arrangers commit to only what they know they can accomplish themselves. Notice how quickly memory boards and memory tables became a standard at almost every funeral; that's because the funeral director could promise these to a family without risk. If the family brings the items in, the funeral director will make them part of the visitation and funeral.

Before the advent of DVD when video tributes were shipped from the producer to the funeral home via overnight service relatively few funeral homes offered them. It wasn't until funeral homes began producing DVD tributes in-house that they really caught on. Today nearly every funeral home in the country offers DVD tributes.

If the arranger interests a family in a special product or service, particularly any product or service that is dependent upon a shipping service (Fed Ex or UPS) for the delivery of an engraved urn, custom printed product such as a portrait or custom created casket panel insert, there is always the risk the provider or the shipping service will fail to deliver. Think about it; a national shipping service would be very proud of a 95% success rate for overnight delivery, but what funeral home owner would be satisfied with a funeral director that disappointed 5% of the families they served? In fact, the two major overnight services have a 75% on-time record for morning delivery, probably very good for overnight delivery, but hardly adequate for a funeral director.

Mondays are the busiest day for funerals, and a lot of the arrangements for Monday funerals are made on Friday, or even Saturday morning. If the family orders a custom product, such as a photo montage, the arranger will need the photos at the funeral home early enough to scan the photos and email them to the specialty print lab early enough for the product to be created and delivered to the shipping service in time to be shipped for delivery Saturday morning for a 10:00 AM service. If the arrangements are made on Saturday, then the product certainly can not be ordered; if the family gets the photos to the funeral home too late on Friday afternoon, the printed product won't be available for Monday.

The point is, the arranger has too many details to address during a two-hour arrangement session to consider all of the shipping specifications and product requirements for them to confidently commit to a family that it will be delivered on time for a service.

Why should the funeral director take that risk? Presenting add on products and services seldom ever impacts their earnings; even if incentives are included in their compensation package, the commission from the sale of a jewelry or printed item is insufficient to make a visible impact on their income. Since most of the specialty products available to funeral home customers are unknown to the public, family members do not anticipate a presentation of special products. Funeral arrangers are rewarded for doing just what families expect of them; as a result there is no incentive for the to accept the risk of going any further.

What's Wrong With This Situation?

The national economy is in a deep recession that has made consumers reticent to make large purchases. But the recession will pass, whether sooner or later, the consumer will return; but will the funeral customer return?

The baby boomer generation has been severely stung by this recession; their homes are worth less than they planned, and their 401K's have been devastated. When the economy returns to normal it won't be lead by baby boomer spending, instead their children and grand children will return to the auto dealers and home centers. If funerals and memorial services continue to be routine and uneventful, Baby Boomers may very well conclude they are an unnecessary expense.

Another contributing factor to the decline in the funeral industry is the very low death rate. The national birth rate began to decline in 1930 along with the economy. Birth rates were low throughout the depression and didn't return to pre-depression era levels until 1945; it wasn't until the 1950's that the birthrate began its precipitous incline. Given a projected life span of 80 years, the 1945-generation won't begin dying in large numbers till 2015; but a visible increase in the number of deaths won't occur until 2025. So for funeral service, this recession could easily endure another 15 years.

As the cremation rate continues its incessant growth, funeral service profitability will be dependent upon add-on sales. Delivering meaningful, personalized and memorable services is dependent upon consumers investing in the experience. Creating experiences means funeral arrangers need to inform families of all the available options; which means they must take the risk inherent in offering products that cannot be produced or inventoried in-house.

Funeral home owners and managers must accept the fact that some families will be aggravated or irritated when arrangers present personalization and memorial products. Think of it this way; how many products purchased at department stores are returned; and that happens when the purchaser examined the product and even tried it on in the dressing room.

Customer satisfaction surveys must be truly analyzed; it's not just a matter of reading the raw score. Some families are determined to be dissatisfied even before they arrive at the funeral home. When a survey evaluates every aspect of a funeral business poorly, beginning with the funeral facility exterior and interior, staff, arranger and every facet of the service is unsatisfactory, it has to be assumed the person making the evaluation was prejudiced against funeral service, or the firm, or even the fact that the rest of the family wanted a funeral.

Summary: It's very easy to criticize an arranger for making routine arrangements and selling the same merchandise over and over. It is far more difficult for owners and managers to be self-critical for not creating an environment where arrangers can be successful.

Dr. Thomas Shaw, a professor in the Southern Illinois University school of Mortuary Science is conducting a long term Funeral Director Inventory study to identify personality traits that contribute to success as a funeral director. One of his findings to date is that funeral directors a strong at following routine; such as directing ceremony and practicing a technical process (such as embalming). Translating this to the arrangement room, funeral directors should receive specific training as to how to use specific arrangement tools then encouraged to repeat these processes.

Also, funeral arrangers should be rewarded for risk taking when attempting to accomplish a business objective. If the firm has an objective to make memorial services more personalized, and the arranger presents personalization to the family, there should be some means of recognizing the effort even if the family does not make a purchase. Funeral arrangers cannot control what a family does, only what they do. A batter in a baseball game can do everything right and still strike out but when players do the right things consistently, they become consistent hitters. Arrangers should be rewarded for making the effort not just when they get a hit.

CHAPTER 28

The Business Perspective of Personalization

For the past decade, funeral homes have been experimenting with personalization. Video tributes were introduced in the late 1980's; memory tables, photographs and non-traditional music are increasingly common.

Experts estimate 40% of all funerals and memorials include some element of personalization. MKJ conducted focus groups in December of 2000 with randomly selected Floridians, age 35+. A majority of the respondents had attended funerals that diminished the religious influences and elevated personalization. The general consensus from the focus groups was that the personalized funerals were more interesting and meaningful than traditional funerals they had attended.

Research conducted for funeral homes nationally by MKJ over the past 18 years indicate an increasing demand for flexibility in funeral services. As the American population has become better educated and more mobile, they have come to be more demanding consumers. Just as restaurants, hotels, automakers, even churches, have had to change to meet society's expectations, so have funeral homes.

As with any successful merchandising concept, the benefits of personalization are multidimensional. Personalization improves merchandise sales by engaging the family in the event. Traditional funeral arrangement focused on administrative and technical issues that focused on the funeral directors knowledge and authority. Arranging a personalized funeral places the emphasis on the family. They are the authority in defining the life of the deceased. Their input is absolutely necessary for the event to be produced. Their elevated level of involvement carries over to the selection room.

Secondly, personalization expands the product line. Because the family is arranging an event, their personal standards require the funeral home to carry an extended choice of options in products. Traditionally, funeral directors simply provided memory books, memorial cards, and "thank you" cards. When the consumer is making the selection, the product selected reflects their personal taste as opposed to the funeral home's standards.

Third, personalization provides a foundation upon which traditional funeral homes can compete with the spectrum of low-cost alternatives available in most cities. For many funeral homes, the standard fare is a two-hour visitation immediately before the funeral. This simple service can be easily duplicated by the low-cost alternatives at a much lower cost with lower overhead. The standard, simple funeral allows the discount operation to serve more families; the greater volume offsets the lower margins. If this situation persists, traditional funeral homes will be forced to lower their prices to that of the discounters.

Personalization requires greater effort than discount firms will be able to devote to each funeral. The greater service, larger inventory of products, the time involved in making arrangements, preparing for the visitations and funerals will be difficult for discount operations to duplicate.

Fourth, personalization increases the consumers' appreciation for funeral home services that will perpetuate the demand. As consumers attend personalized funerals, they will come to expect the higher standard; they will contact those full-service funeral homes that advertise personalized funerals, and where they have attended personalized funerals.

More importantly, personalization appeals to those consumers which have been most difficult for funeral homes to reach. The higher-income, better-educated and less-religious consumer represents the clientele for minimum-service cremation societies and discount death care operations. Research data collected from MKJ research studies indicate the appeal for personalized services is stronger with this group than with the lower-income, lower-educated, more-religious groups which have become the most desirable funeral home customer over the past decade.

"Bowling Alone," a popular management book, details the changing demographics of Americans' participation in society. The book documents how volunteering, civic activity, participation in religious and national issues has diminished steadily since World War II. Even activities such as reading the local newspaper have declined as individuals withdraw from society to focus on career development, personal hobbies (thus bowling alone as opposed to bowling in leagues) and family issues.

"Bowling Alone" has direct implications on the funeral industry, as fewer people feel obligated to attend the funeral of a business or social acquaintance. When they do attend, many people leave with the feeling the ceremony was empty and meaningless. Personalization, through expanded memorial cards featuring personal photographs, and personalized copy discussing the important role the deceased had in the lives of those close to him, allow those in attendance to better appreciate the life which had been lived, and the reason for the ceremony.

MKJ research studies include a question which lists a variety of funeral home services for the purpose of identifying which services the consumer perceives of greatest value. Included in the list are personalized funerals, children's rooms, community rooms, and Web-based services, such as online obituaries, online prearrangement and online purchase of merchandise. Of all of the services listed, personalization was selected as the most important in every study in which the question was included. In most studies, personalization was selected 50% more often than the next most often selected feature (children's rooms).

More importantly, the personalization concept is most popular with hard-to-reach consumers. For example, it is generally accepted the more religious a family, the more likely they will be to have a traditional funeral. In regard to personalization, individuals who indicated they had no religious affiliations are more likely to perceive value in personalization than are those respondents which identified themselves as Catholic or Protestant.

In regard to income, the higher the household income, the more likely they are to state "the availability of personalized funerals would have a strong positive impact on their selection of a funeral home."

In regard to age, the younger the respondent, the more likely they are to indicate personalization would be important to them in the selection of a funeral home.

"Personalized services would have a strong impact on my selection of a funeral home."

Religion:	Catholics		Protestant	None
	40%		44%	45%
Income:	<$25	$25- $40	$40 - $55	>$55
	33%	41%	50%	52%
Age:	<45	45-54	55-64	65+
	59%	51%	37%	25%

Personalization even has significant potential in pre-need sales, as those groups least likely to pre-arrange in the past, perceive the greatest value in personalization. As such, incorporating personalization into the pre-need advertising message has the potential of creating a new pre-need clientele.

Already own a pre-need contract

Age:	55-64	>65
	12.3%	19.3%
Income:	<$25K	>$55K
	23%	9%

MKJ research also indicates a growing propensity to pre-arrange funeral services. The younger the respondent, the more inclined the individual is to plan on making funeral arrangements in the future. (Of course, one reason for this is the older the respondent, the more likely they are to already have made pre-arrangements.) The question is what will these people pre-arrange?

Likely to pre-arrange in the future:

Age	<45	45-54	55-64	65+
	58%	52%	40%	23%

Given the present mindset of higher-income, better-educated, youthful consumers, their pre-arrangements will be minimal. As such, marketing pre-planning to this group could actually have very negative implications on funeral business. Orienting these pre-need prospects to personalized services and involving families in making arrangements as opposed to individuals, will result in better quality sales, as well as more meaningful services.

Summary: The most popular management text of 2000 was the quick read, "Who Moved My Cheese" by Spencer Johnson, PhD., which illustrates, through fantasy, how different personality groups react to change, and how those who adapt most quickly to change reap the greatest awards.

Over the past twenty years, the trend in funeral service, particularly on the west coast, has been to serve more families while profit margins shrink, often times to the point of being negligible. This trend will spread across the U.S. given time. With the huge, aging baby boomer population nearing their sixties, the emphasis in funeral service will shift from the traditional search for volume to building value in each family served. Those funeral firms that accomplish this first will be the death service industry's success stories in the coming decades.

What may be most difficult for practitioners to accept is that personalization of funerals is consistent with traditional funeral service, not a departure. Regional, provincial practices such as hanging crepe on the front doors of families in grief, or displaying a receiver off the hook of an antique phone (illustrating Jesus called and momma answered) are all efforts to personalize funeral services in ways which have meaning to the family. Established customs are easily accomplished because they are traditions deeply rooted in a community's culture. As such, the staff understands them well and accomplishes them routinely.

New programs always represent a challenge simply because they require people to perform their job differently. As such, the funeral director's role has changed, but the objective is the same.

CHAPTER 29

Pre-need Issues

The most pressing question in funeral service is, why are pre-need sales down nationally? Consider the following:

A. The public's confidence in financial institutions is so shaken they feel safer keeping their cash close to them.

B. The public's confidence in the funeral profession is shaken from pre-need and other scandals.

C. The public is so concerned about the economy they don't want to make any large purchases.

D. People don't think about their funerals when they are worried about their job.

Don't even consider "All of the above" as that doesn't help you decide whether to press forward with pre-need or layoff until the public's confidence in funeral service returns.

My personal belief is "C," pre-need sales will return along with public confidence in the economy over the next several years. Focus groups recently conducted by MKJ in a mid-size southern city demonstrated that consumers are knowledgeable of the cremation and pre-need scandals, but the public's view of the funeral profession is similar to how they perceive the U.S. Congress. Most congressmen are corrupt and lazy, but we love our congressmen so much we reelect him time and time again. The scandals upset the public, but they continue to trust their local funeral director.

The economy will improve, but the projections are that it will take a long time. In the mean time, many funeral homes will diminish or drop their pre-need effort simply because their counselors will not be able to generate sufficient commissions. So the question is, what can funeral homes and counselors do during these challenging months?

The answer is, business as usual, but different.

Many counselors believe pre-need cannot be sold in December, as families do not want to think about funerals while preparing for Christmas. To overcome this, many funeral firms will contact families that met with them throughout the year but decided not to make a purchase at that time. The appeal is a simple one; "This being the end of the year ,we are reevaluating our prices. If you choose to prepay your arrangements before the end of the year, it will be at this year's price; if you wait until January the new price schedule will be in force and your cost will be higher." With this kind of appeal, December can become a very good pre-need sales month.

In that same way, recessions have always represented a pre-need sales opportunity. A common objection to prepaying funeral arrangements is that other investment options grow faster than pre-need insurance policies or bank trust accounts. During a recession, when people are losing money in the stock market and money market accounts and CDs are paying minimal returns, a pre-need policy's set return looks more attractive. Contacting people that have money in other investments can prove a productive prospecting effort.

Certainly generating sales is always a challenge, but there is a much more fundamental issue funeral home owners are considering relative to their pre-need programs; whether or not to guarantee the price. Freezing funeral costs is one factor some consumers consider when pre-paying arrangements, but do the additional sales generated from price guarantees offset the losses incurred at time of need when the death benefit falls short of current funeral costs? Funeral homes nationally are losing as much as $1500 on individual funerals; is there sufficient market share gain to offset these losses?

As with many business decisions, sometimes no decision is the best. Whether or not guaranteeing the price is important is a decision the buyer should be making; not the funeral home owner. Every pre-need contract should include two initial blocks where the consumer designates whether they want to guarantee the price today or make other decisions at time of need. I am not an attorney, and do not present the following as appropriate verbiage for an agreement, but simply a generalization of what an agreement might specify.

> I understand that this agreement does not freeze the cost of my funeral and that my family may have to make additional decisions at the time of my death to either pay additional funds or choose fewer services or other merchandise.

> I do not want my family to have to pay any additional costs at the time of my death. For that reason, I am purchasing a larger pre-need contract today than would be necessary to meet the cost of my funeral at the current prices. If the insurance policy death benefits are greater than the amount needed to pay for my arrangements and merchandise based upon funeral costs at the time of my death, the surplus will be returned to my family by check, or they may choose to use the excess funds for additional services or merchandise.

Giving the consumer the option, relieves the funeral home owner from making a policy decision, and allows the family to make a decision that best fits their situation.

Another pre-need issue that deserves thought is how great an impact pre-need really has on market share? In the very early days of pre-need, when most funeral homes did not offer the service, those few that did realized significant market share gains as families felt it necessary to go to the firm that advertised the service in the belief that most funeral homes did not. But that was decades ago, and today most consumers know that all funeral homes offer pre-need. In fact, consumers are more likely to believe a funeral home offers pre-need than they are to believe the funeral business provides cremation services.

Pre-need represents the death care industry's greatest advertising success story. With nearly every funeral business in the country advertising pre-need, the consumer came to learn the value of the concept very quickly. In contrast, cremation advertising continues to build volume because so many funeral businesses are still reticent to advertise cremation services for fear that burial families will chose cremation instead of traditional funeral services. There is no basis for this concern as any family that wants cremation certainly knows the service is available nearly everywhere. Not advertising the availability of cremation simply drives the business to a competitor.

Returning to pre-need; with the consumer knowing that every funeral home offers pre-need, it is unlikely the investment in pre-need sales and advertising increases market share. It is more likely that families first select the funeral home they want to use, and then decides whether or not to make arrangements in advance. Then they decide whether or not to pre-pay.

The most common form of pre-need advertising in recent years has been the ubiquitous pre-need letter. Typically mass mailed to a list provided by a pre-need insurance company or a third-party sales company, these letters are completely void of any advertising to influence the consumer as to what funeral home to use. Instead, the letter is dependent upon the name of the funeral home for its credibility and relevance. The objective of the letter is not to convince families that one funeral home is better than another, but to simply exploit the funeral home's name and heritage to generate leads. The sterility of this form of lead generation is the strongest argument that pre-need is no longer an effective means of building market share. There is no question that pre-need locks in preference; in fact, pre-need is the most effective defense against low cost alternatives (discounters); but for building market share, maybe not.

Summary: Funeral service is redefining pre-need, just as the nation's financial policies, housing and auto industries are being redefined.

What form will pre-need take?

- Many funeral businesses are exploring end-of-life expense insurance policies, and investigating new techniques of merchandising pre-need.
- Can funeral homes afford a pre-need sales force, or is the concept of an army of counselors swarming over a community passé?
- Are the products designed decades ago when inflation was under control still viable in a period when rampant inflation is projected for the next decade?
- One of the primary sources of pre-need purchases is seniors paying down their personal finances as the move into care facilities. Will this continue to be necessary in a nation with national healthcare?

Are we at the precipice of a return to what pre-need was originally; a convenience funeral businesses offered consumers that wanted to make decisions in advance and approached the funeral home much as they did on an at-need basis?

Selecting a Pre-need Selling Company

Most independent funeral homes became interested in pre-need sales and marketing in the late 1970's or early 80's. Until then, most funeral homes simply met the needs of individual families when they contacted the funeral home. Pre-need didn't become a proactive marketing initiative until competitors, particularly SCI, forced them to address pre-need for what it was, a marketing strategy for building and holding at-need volume.

By the 1990's, most family funeral homes had experimented with pre-need, and for the most part, the funeral homes with meaningful sales were those few firms that had found, and were able to hold, a pre-need salesperson. Ironically, the primary challenge for most funeral homes in 1980 continues to be the primary challenge today; finding someone to sell for you.

For proactive funeral businesses, particularly those in competitive markets, pre-need is a necessary element of a comprehensive marketing strategy; without a pre-need strategy, a funeral business will lose ground over time. This was demonstrated in a recent research study conducted by MKJ Marketing in a mid-size Ohio community where 14% of everyone in the market age 45+ owned a pre-need contract. However, only 4% of the families preferring one of the well-established firms owned a pre-need. This particular firm has experienced consistent decline in their at-need volume over the past decade, including advertising pre-need or employing an active salesperson. Funeral businesses that actively promote themselves, also tend to have an active pre-need sales effort. Those that do not promote pre-need, typically do a very poor job at promoting their firm in general.

There is an alternative to managing an in-house pre-need sales force; over the past twenty years a number of pre-need selling companies have developed in the deathcare industry. The reputations for these companies vary widely, but for the most part, many funeral homes are leery of contracting with a third-party sales company because they are afraid of turning over their business reputation and image in the community to another business. Funeral homes have good reason for being concerned; a pre-need sales company that practices counterproductive sales tactics can seriously damage a funeral home's reputation. At the same time, a third-party selling company that does little, will produce little, in which case the funeral business will suffer in the long term as their competitors pull ahead of them in pre-need sales.

Almost all pre-need salespeople will have a 50% close rate; very high compared to life insurance, security systems, or other products and services sold in the home. The close rate is high because most people inherently see the logic of funeral pre-planning. The challenge in selling pre-need is not closing; it's getting into the home. Pre-need sales people cause problems for the funeral home when they become too aggressive at appointment setting. Getting an appointment and getting the family to keep the appointment is the greatest challenge. So, if you are considering a third-party selling company, the first question you want to ask is *"how will you generate leads?"*

The most productive promotional effort any funeral home can engage in is public relations. Simply put, consumers like knowing someone at the funeral home; in fact knowing a staff member at a funeral home is the second most often volunteered reason for preferring a funeral home (past experience is the most often volunteered factor given by research respondents, and it is reasonable to expect anyone that used a funeral home in the past would remember somebody on the funeral home staff they could contact if a death occurred in their family).

Most funeral homes are involved in some type of public relations efforts, if only to purchase advertising space in the high school yearbooks, church bulletin ads, or some other passive means of participating in the community. Certainly, the most productive public relations is having intelligent, professional individuals making public relations presentations, and participating in local civic events. These public relations efforts are also the best means of generating pre-need leads. Good pre-need selling companies are those that train their sales counselors how to be productive public relations representatives for the funeral homes they represent. These events allow them to become personally identified as a knowledgeable professional representing a quality institution; the local funeral home.

By implementing a public relations lead generating effort, the cost of lead generation is held well below the cost of advertising-generated leads which assures both parties a financially successful relationship. By scheduling many events throughout the year, the lead flow is continuous and fresh, meaning the prospect is seriously thinking about pre-need having just learned of their options, and is mentally ready to move ahead.

Although most pre-need selling companies are familiar with the concept of generating pre-need sales through public relations, few have actually structured their operation to make their public relations efforts productive. There are two keys to making this strategy work; the pre-need sales company must invest in training and in developing public information programs; neither of which is simple or inexpensive.

According to surveys, public speaking is the greatest fear in America; not all qualified salespeople have the personal confidence or capabilities to make good presentations. And even if the individual is comfortable making a presentation, it doesn't mean they would be capable of developing the script and graphics for a program. If the pre-need sales company says they will use public relations programs to generate pre-need leads, have them bring one of their counselors to your funeral home to make a presentation. Don't have the owner or sales manager make the presentation, have a salesperson that is working for one of their funeral home clients make the presentation. Chances are they won't have a counselor that can make a good presentation simply because most of them don't really use public relations as much as they say they do.

If a counselor does make a sample presentation, have your family and staff sit through the presentation, and ask them how they would respond to the speaker. *"Would you buy pre-need from this individual having just seen this presentation?"* Chances are the nays will outnumber the yes votes. Most pre-need salespeople that try to make productive presentations do not have the tools available to them to be effective. Today's consumer expects a professional presentation to be professional; to include PowerPoint slides, or active video to facilitate communication. Most pre-need salespeople will use no audio/ visual aids or amateurish word slides that the speaker simply reads to the audience as if they were illiterate or blind. Word slides do not represent effective graphics; they're insulting and boring. Effective graphics make the message more easily understood as opposed to simply being notes for the speaker's benefit.

Another factor to consider when selecting a pre-need sales company is how the salesperson will be recruited and prepared for their new position. *"Who is going to train this person to be my pre-need sales counselor?"* A professional sales company will have an experienced recruiter, and a trainer with extensive experience developing pre-need sales counselors out of both funeral directors and non-funeral directors. They will understand the strengths the individual should have developed from previous employment, and know how to fill in the gaps to make them productive in pre-need. Be careful if the same person that presented the company to you, is also the recruiter and trainer; it is highly unlikely that individual will be as good at all of those functions as they think they are. They problem is, neither you nor the salesperson will appreciate their weaknesses until they are in the field trying to create leads and appointments.

A fundamental requirement for any pre-need counselor is for them to live in the community in which they are selling. If they live in the community, they will also go to church in the community, which is a primary source for pre-need and at-need sales. Also, a local person will be more sensitive to how they relate to prospects since their reputation is on the line, just as the funeral firm's.

A pre-need sales company should have established reporting procedures to keep you apprised of their productivity in your firm's behalf. How many leads are they generating, how many resulted in appointments, and how many sold through? When a family decided not to purchase a pre-need contract, what follow-up tools do they have in place to keep the relationship alive until the family does decide to move ahead?

One of the best means of evaluating a pre-need sales company is to study the insurance companies they represent. How many companies do they work with, and are they nationally recognized. A pre-need company should be affiliated with a number of insurance companies. The more companies they work with, they better suited the insurance product will be to your particular needs. Also, the insurance company should not be selected based upon commission rates alone; you want insurance companies that offer diverse products. Most pre-need insurance companies provide a guaranteed product that will insure anyone, but these products represent a very bad investment for healthy applicants; as such, it is good to have multiple products.

The highest commissions are paid when the family opts for an extended payment period, but this typically results in the family paying much more than the face value of the funeral due to carrying charges. Funeral home owners should be very cautious if more than 25% of the pre-need contracts sold are using extended payment terms. Families will often stop making payments when they realize how much they are paying, and resent the funeral home for getting them involved in such a bad deal. Also, some sales counselors will sell the family on an extended payment schedule; collect the higher commission, only to have arranged with the family in advance to pay off the contract early in the payment schedule shortly after the higher commission is received. Obviously this is not favorable to the insurance company, but it's also not good for the funeral home's image as the family pays too much, and they get the feeling they were involved in something that wasn't completely above board. Again, not good for the funeral home's image.

Summary: Most funeral homes have very good reputations locally; one of the means of benefiting from this good reputation is by selling pre-need. Just because the owners or managers are uncomfortable hiring, training, and supervising a sales effort doesn't mean they should not have a program. Pre-need selling companies represent a very viable option for most funeral homes; but just as careful funeral home managers closely scrutinize the crematory services they patronize, and the casket companies they buy from, they should also study the pre-need sales companies they use

CHAPTER 30

Pricing for today's funeral consumer

What is the root cause of the current turbulence in the American automobile industry? Is it high manufacturing cost, or the consumers' difficulty in getting financing for a car loan? Or is it a simpler explanation? On a recent visit to Los Angeles I waited on a busy corner and had an opportunity to notice the traffic; out of hundreds of vehicles the only American made cars were a few large SUV's. The great majority of the vehicles are small, high quality, fuel efficient European and Asian cars, and its been this way in California for the past 20 years.

Marketers since the 1960's have looked to the west for emerging trends in fashion, design, entertainment; nearly every facet of American life. How could the American auto manufacturers have missed the obvious signs of a consumer trend away from large vehicles to European and Asian designed models? They didn't miss it; they chose to ignore it because short term profits were better rehashing old designs and popular SUV's.

Would it have been possible for the auto companies to taken advantage of the opportunity the popularity of the SUV's and large sedans offered while also building a foundation for the future vehicles? Sure; in the 1970's and 80's and 90's, the big three were three were among the largest most profitable corporations in the world; they could have done anything they set their mind to.

Why rehash this well worn story? Because the funeral profession is committing the same terminal mistake:

- How many funeral directors are receiving cremation arrangement training?
- How many staff members know how to constructively take a price shoppers call?
- How many funeral homes offer food service in the funeral home?
- Of the funeral homes with catering services, how many have presentation tools to help the arrangers present this new service?

The funeral industry is compressing; for the first time in history the number of funeral homes in the US is actually declining. Funeral home owners are taking aggressive steps to maintain their profits; not the high profits of the 60's and 70's, but the lower profits of the late 90's. Imported caskets, pet crematories and other efforts to generate profits avoid the true challenge; how to retool a burial based industry to a cremation based industry.

83% of consumers that want ground burial already own their cemetery property. Because so many seniors already own cemetery property, ground burial continues as the most preferred form of disposition. But the huge baby boomer generation is becoming the prime death market and they don't own cemetery property; even more significantly they have children in college, they don't have retirement plans like their parents, and they don't have job security during their final working years. It is simply fantasy to assume these people will add cemetery property to their financial "to do" list during their retirement years. It is impossible to use any algorithm to project how quickly the cremation rate is going to increase in the second half of the next decade.

From a competitive perspective, the decline in burial could mean a competitive advantage for stand alone funeral homes in competition with combinations, but that won't be sufficient to offset the higher profits derived from ground burial. Take a few minutes to do some simple financial analysis:

- Compute your average profits from a ground burial
- Compute your profits from your cremation business

If you're like most funeral homes, your burial business is subsidizing your cremation business; but what's going to subsidize the cremation business when it represents 80% of your volume?

But that's not the real problem. The greater challenge will be to re-orient the public to the prices funeral homes will have to charge for cremation services when burial is no longer common. Cremation charges are ridiculously low; in many markets a minimum cremation costs less than dinner for two at a typical steak house.

Traditionally funeral homes created a product for the average consumer. It was based upon the concept that most families wanted pretty much the same type of services. Even today, most funeral homes have a standard service charge. The problem is there is no standard funeral consumer, which leaves families looking for the firm they think best serves their needs as opposed to asking the funeral director what the firm can do for them.

When the consumer observes competition in an industry it causes them to become more demanding. They see lower priced funeral homes advertising their prices, and they realize they are in control. When they telephone a funeral home to compare prices, what they are really doing is shopping services. They want to know how flexible you can be and whether your services meet their needs. That's why it's important to offer packages. Packages communicate choices and options; and that's what today's consumers' want.

Most funeral homes serve communities. Maybe the community is a stand alone town or city, or maybe it's a specific segment of a major metro area. In either case most of a funeral firms business will come from a relatively tight radius; sometimes as few as two zip codes, sometimes as many as ten. In either case, there are not enough families in that radius to segment the market. Most funeral homes want to serve any one and everyone within that radius. To do that you first have to realize not every family will want the same thing. Quoting a family a standard service charge is in effect telling that they have to conform to your system as opposed to the funeral firm conforming to their needs.

A Three-step Process for Increasing Revenues

Asking yourself "What can I do to increase revenue?" is part and parcel of running any business. Literally hundreds of concepts for new products and services have been proposed to the industry to be merchandised through funeral homes over the past twenty years. Today, funeral home owners and managers are more receptive to new products and services as consumers are less receptive to the traditional offerings; but how do we decide which ideas to pursue and which to reject? What is the yardstick for measuring the viability of a new product or service?

In reality, the decision making process is simple; it becomes complicated when we allow our prejudices to cloud our decision making. Funeral businesses have often rationalized large investments in new business concepts simply because we want to do something different; other times we reject viable concepts because implementation seems too difficult.

Hundreds of funeral businesses have ventured into the cemetery business or built new facilities without performing due diligence, and have lived to regret their decisions. When making a significant business decision, it is important to remember that wanting to be successful doesn't make it so. All of the hard work in the world can't make a bad decision work. Nonetheless, funeral home revenues are diminishing, making it absolutely necessary for us to consider new business opportunities. When making these decisions consider the following:

Pursue Superior Profits: Most of the business opportunities considered by small business owners have little opportunity to generate meaningful profits. There are many opportunities for generating marginal profits; any business broker can introduce you to hundreds of marginally successful businesses. A good example is the minimal cremation business; it's too crowded to actually create good income, labor and advertising costs are high, and they typically fail to build customer loyalty. Another example is cremation jewelry; certainly there is some demand for these products, and funeral homes should offer them. But be realistic; at the end of the year, the additional revenues generated by these ancillary sales will be negligible. The greatest benefit from offering these products is that it communicates to the public your willingness to look for new ways to memorialize.

Too many funeral businesses entered pre-need as a business venture as opposed to seeing it for what it is, a marketing concept for building at-need business. As with any marketing program, pre-need costs the firm to maintain. When managed correctly, it can create additional volume and insurance commissions will offset much of the cost; but as an enterprise, pre-need cannot sustain itself as a stand-alone business.

Maintain Focus: Opportunities exist in death care services to generate superior profits. Business consultants and academicians maintain a common theme on the topic of expansion; whether large enterprises or small, companies should focus their resources on their primary business. Few small business owners have sufficient cash, human resources or business expertise to venture far from their primary business; and when they do, their primary business typically suffers.

Limit Up-front Investment: When investing in new concepts or businesses, large corporations first start small so as to limit their risk, and incorporate the new venture as a separate entity to protect the core business from liability in the event the new venture fails.

Being small business owners, even a relatively small up-front cost can have long-term ramifications on a family's financial stability. Small business owners typically use their own cash or personal debt to make investments; as such, it is impossible to insulate yourself from liability.

Using the above criteria, what opportunities can we identify for funeral homes to increase revenues? What new products and services can we offer that fall within these criteria:

1. Have the potential to create superior profits
2. Support the primary business
3. Require limited up-front investment

Two opportunities come immediately to mind:

- Special services to individualize the funeral
- Food service

Special Services

For most funeral homes, personalization is a matter of remodeling the casket selection room, and merchandising add-on products, such as corner ornaments, head panel portraits and other artwork. Both of which are necessary and productive; but they are just the beginning of the process of individualizing the funeral. Further, given the increasing competition from online casket stores, the opportunity for superior profits from merchandise sales is limited.

The best new source of additional revenues for funeral homes is to merchandise those products and services only funeral homes can provide. When a family selects an additional service, such as a butterfly release, piper musical program, dove release, military ceremony, or other special musical program, the additional revenues generated by the funeral home can be outstandingly profitable, since there is seldom any significant additional cost involved. Also, families are unlikely to shop other sources for these special services.

Special services that individualize the funeral, support the primary business by enhancing the value received by the family served, as well as educating those in attendance as to the relevance of a funeral.

Special services typically require little or no up-front investment other than arranger training, and this investment returns very high profits both in terms of improved sales, and in the personal satisfaction derived by the professional staff. Funeral directors want to be productive, both for their employer and the consuming public. When they possess the communication skills necessary to arrange a special service, they understand their role within their funeral firm, as well as their role in society.

Food Service

As long as there have been funerals, there has been some type of reception. Traditionally, these receptions have occurred in a family member's home or the church of the deceased. Increasingly, Americans are unchurched, and contemporary families are often scattered. Death often occurs in retirement villages or nursing homes, leaving no appropriate, private location for a reception following funerals. As such, families often find themselves negotiating with banquet halls and directing friends and family members to drive across town in hectic traffic in order to receive the support people in grief are wanting and are supposed to be receiving from the funeral process.

Many funeral facilities presently have rooms that would easily accommodate receptions, either in their existing facilities, or in neighboring buildings. Many funeral businesses own homes adjacent to their funeral facilities that could easily be remodeled into a reception facility. Presenting three or four levels of food services offered by a local caterer would be considered helpful by most families, and would represent a new source of income. Certainly, offering food service is no more a stretch for most funeral homes than offering floral selections provided by a local florist, monuments, or even vaults. The only difference is flowers, monuments, and vaults are products most funeral directors are comfortable with, and food represents a new venture.

Because relationship building is job one for any funeral home, the benefits of having an opportunity for the arranging funeral director, or owner, to socialize with families following a funeral would likely be more productive at building future at-need volume than aggressively selling pre-need services.

For most firms, the greatest challenge to operating a reception facility could be parking when families remain on the premises hours following a funeral. Certainly, this is a consideration for no more than 15% of the funeral firms nationally. But when the cost of additional parking is compared against the superior profits that can be generated from a reception hall and the competitive advantage it affords a funeral home, this is certainly a viable solution that would not incur an unreasonable investment.

CHAPTER 31

The Incongruity of Funeral Service

Funeral service often defies analogies with other businesses and industries. Most business concepts are developed with a specific demographic group in mind:

- McDonald's is inexpensive dining.
- Chevrolet is vehicles for mid-income consumers.
- Ritz is for the wealthy. Wealthy are comfortable paying more for exclusivity.

Funeral services are relatively expensive, but increasingly, affluent consumers reject higher-priced funeral home services, preferring the exclusivity of a reception at their yacht club, country club or community center.

Consumer research suggests consumers are beginning to sense this incongruity as mid and lower-income families increasingly challenge traditional values and consider alternatives.

To create a strategy to win back the mass market, we should first understand how mid-income families came to invest a disproportionate amount of family resources in funeral services.

The popular theme, "Tipping Point" suggests that trends and fads are initiated by individuals in search of ways to be different. These people are not leaders, in fact, they resent others who copy their unusual behavior. Nonetheless, others do pick up on their contrarian behavior, and over time, what began as aberrant becomes a fad, and can become a trend. In the early 1900's, it was very unusual to prefer cremation, and for many, the option was not practical since there were few crematoriums. The practice was so rare, those preferring it created societies to assure their wishes would be carried out.

No one would have thought such a beginning would lead to a 30% national cremation rate.

The fad became a trend in the 1970's and 80's as well-educated consumers began to defect from the established norm. The most desirable funeral service clientele, the "carriage trade" of the 1940's, 50's and 60's, came to prefer a minimalist service.

The loss of the carriage trade was accepted by funeral homes nationally as they began to focus their attention on the far larger mid-income demographics. Mid-income families were relatively simple to serve. In contrast to the demanding, high-income consumer, blue-collar families will accept a lower level of individual attention. They simply want to be like everyone else, making them easy to serve and very profitable. But the mid-income group is beginning to notice that affluent consumers are no longer having grand services.

The popularity of cremation is growing faster than CANA projects. Based upon research studies conducted by MKJ Marketing, the national cremation rate could reach 50% within 15 years, several decades sooner than projected by CANA. Why?

The primary point of the "Tipping Point" is that the following for a trend compounds as it becomes more common. As more people select cremation, more people will be influenced to do the same until such point it becomes the norm. Funeral service marketing efforts, such as pre-planned funerals and funeral home Web sites will contribute to this process. Increasingly, people are pre-planning lower cost services. Certainly the funeral home appreciates the prearrangement, but often the prearrangements are at a value lower than the firm's at-need average. Successful discount operations' first signs of success are in their pre-need sales. Emailed condolences allow friends and acquaintances to avoid the unpleasant social responsibility of attending a funeral, or even sending a card.

As the cremation rate has grown, funeral homes have made adjustments. In fact, funeral homes have adjusted better than the cemetery, casket, vault, or even urn companies. In fact, funeral homes have adapted too well.

At 10% cremation rate, owners' income expectations were diminished. Owners made less money, but the business continued.

At 20% the consolidation process began allowing those unable to change to exit the profession, and acquirers to replace smaller margins with increased volume.

At 30%, the consolidation pace will be even greater, but the purchase prices will be far lower as acquirers will know how difficult it is to run a larger business and that profits will be slim. It will become a buyers' market and buyers will be very particular.

At 50%, death care in the U.S. will be redefined. Bronze and copper caskets will be as rare as silver deposit caskets are today. As opposed to 22,000 funeral rooftops nationally, there will be 10,000. The majority of the population will choose disposition services with a minority opting for funerals held in traditional funeral homes.

Just as the Ritz, Mercedes, Rolex and other exclusive products realize profits by charging higher prices, the remaining funeral homes will be expensive and profitable; and their services will be very personal. The surviving funeral businesses will be determined in the coming decade; they will be the ones that make intelligent acquisitions, build strong brand names and learn to treat each family individually versus just another family with a dead relative.

CHAPTER 32

Marketing Objectives For the New Economy

Point of purchase merchandising in the arrangement process. An emphasis on serving the family is wonderful, and should be the priority at every funeral home. However, many funeral directors have come to believe serving the family means not presenting personalization options with the same excuse of they don't want to become salespeople. No consumer is well served when the knowledgeable professional they consult fails to provide important information. Personalization and memorialization are what families come to funeral homes for; not educating the consumer is failing at job one.

Accept that success in funeral business will be (or is) dependent upon profiting from cremation. Small business owners are very consistent in how they respond to challenges. We tend to be very pragmatic when responding to urgent situations, whether opportunities or threats to our business. Small business owners can be very creative and generate tremendous short-term energy when addressing a short-term objective.

Funeral home owner's attitudes regarding facilities are a good example. As a local businessperson, most funeral home owners maintain cognizance of what's happening in their community. They keep a close eye on the maintenance of their existing facilities, and will typically take action long before a physical weakness in their buildings becomes a major problem. They look at growing neighborhoods as potential locations for new buildings; they watch particular lots and are proactive in making moves to secure property for the future buildings. They observe growing ethnic populations and make contacts within those communities to gain a foothold on future business.

On the other hand, small businesses typically do not respond well to long-term challenges. We watch a situation unfold over many years without taking effective action simply because the challenge never rises to a level of urgency that demands a specific reaction.

The cremation challenge is an excellent example. Funeral home owners have watched as the cremation rate has increased from 2% to 5%, 10%, 20%, even 50% in some markets and owners have watched as their profit margins have declined as a result of cremation, but most have not taken a pragmatic approach to resolving the problem. And for good reasons; the cremation challenge cannot be resolved quickly. There is no simple, specific response that will put the problem behind us. The cremation challenge will exist as long as there are funeral homes. Becoming a cremation-oriented funeral home requires sustained focus; it necessitates management reconsider every facet of the funeral firm's operation, including staff training, arrangement procedures, first call, promotional efforts and messages, safety and operational procedures.

As with most significant social trends, cremation began in the far west, Florida and select metro areas, primarily those near coast lines, and began its move toward the center of the country. The funeral practitioners in the initial areas did not proactively respond to the challenge simply because they didn't see it coming and did not appreciate the potential impact. As a result, cremation has done near fatal damage to traditional funeral homes in these areas. The death care industry in Los Angeles is polarized between very large combinations and minimal cremation businesses; both of which can do very well financially with volume. The remnants of what was once a thriving traditional funeral business survives by specializing in ethnic groups, isolated communities and cost control. There is no structural obstacle in place in most states to preclude this evolution from occurring nationally.

Whenever small business owners feel challenged, they tend to look to one another for answers and solutions. This occurred with pre-need, the FTC, OSHA, and when other industry-wide or regional challenges manifested. Many funeral homes have concluded that " if you can't beat them, join them" and have created their own minimal cremation businesses, with mixed results. Neither of these reactions can be truly successful because they will not transform a traditional funeral home into a cremation-oriented death care business. Only by making structural changes in the way a funeral home does business can cremation become a constructive product.

- Install a crematory.

- Conduct crematory tours and seminars.
- Co-sponsor columbarium projects with churches, clubs, schools, etc.
- Include the word "cremation" on signage.

Sponsor VIP open house events and receptions with professional development programs featuring recognized authorities for:

- Hospice nurses
- EMS
- Police
- Nursing home staff
- Clergy

Senior public relations. Knowing a staff member is the second most common reason for preferring a funeral home.

- Senior trips are a great way for seniors to build identity with your firm and staff.
- Recognizing Veterans: It is often said that SCI is a company with 1000 great ideas but unable to execute. The exception is their traveling Vietnam memorial wall, which they have been doing for well over a decade. Veterans represent the foundation of funeral services as the spouse would be inclined to contact a funeral home with veterans' services, and her children will likely take her to the same place.

Building a quality brand is a matter of time, but also influenced by the messages consumers receive from your firm. When the public encounters staff members active in the community, they come to believe the firm is concerned.

There is a popular, summer reading book entitled, *"All I Really Need to Know I Learned in Kindergarten."* The premise is simple enough; the book describes the fundamentals for human interaction by relating them to playground experiences. Although this is not an endorsement for the book, it effectively demonstrates how fundamentally simple life can be when we don't complicate it with ancillary priorities. We typically recognize the big decisions for what they are; we know when the roof needs replacing, not because it is actively leaking, but because we know that it soon will. Most of us know what we are trying to accomplish in raising children, managing household finances, and running our businesses; major decisions are based upon an underlying philosophy and long-term objectives.

We know when an employee needs disciplining, when we should reserve cash, or make a large investment in our businesses. The problem isn't that we don't know what to do; the problem often is having the discipline and commitment to follow our instincts. Instead we often ignore our best instincts, and move in an opposite direction even when we know it's the wrong thing to do.

Many marginal small businesses ultimately succeed, not because they have a great location or special insight into their business that competitors lacked or any other tangible advantage, except that they are able to maintain discipline in decision making over a long period of time. As opposed to talking themselves out of doing the right thing, they recognize what needs to be done, and execute.

Sometimes we opt for the more expeditious, or the easier, quick fix. Hundreds and hundreds of funeral home owners have told me they know the contributions they make to local groups do nothing for their business, and that they really can't afford to give money away; yet most funeral homes are an easy touch for fundraisers. It is easier to write the check than it is to say no.

Because humans are fallible, the idiom, "plan the work and work the plan" remains relevant and pertinent. We tend to be candid with ourselves when "planning the work." Because "planning" is a cerebral process, it's possible to isolate ourselves from our weaknesses and inefficiencies. Plans look great on paper because they reflect what we know we should do.

Execution can be difficult because "working the plan" demands discipline; sometimes the plan requires us to be leaders, and leading can be hard.

Maintaining Discipline in Advertising

Much of the advertising industry is based upon impulse buying. Radio stations, novelty companies, calendar printers, charities, etc. all package their presentations to get you to make an impulsive decision to incorporate whatever it is they are selling in your ad budget. Because most small business owners and managers are more inclined to meet with a salesperson than they are to create an advertising plan, the salesperson has the upper hand. Because there is no advertising plan in place, anything the salesperson proposes makes sense; the logic runs something like this: *"If I'm not doing anything else, doing something must be better."*

The reality is most funeral home budgets cannot accommodate impulse spending; advertising decisions made without a plan is how funeral homes end up with storage rooms full of stuff they can't remember why they bought, and have no idea how to make productive. So it sits there collecting dust until someone decides to throw it away to make room for something else.

Advertising companies, including MKJ, offer package prices for standard newspaper advertisements; such as ten ads for $850. The reality is very few funeral homes need ten newspaper ads; newspaper media has become so expensive, most funeral homes could not afford the media to run ten newspaper ads an adequate number of times for the consumer to learn the message of each. When a funeral home purchases a large number of advertisements, they are signaling that they have no advertising priorities, and no plan. They don't know why people use them, and why they don't. They have no idea what they are attempting to communicate to their community, as such any advertisement is a good advertisement. And while the advertisements themselves are probably very attractive, well designed with good copy, the real question is whether this advertisement makes a constructive comment about your business.

Every business model should have a unique selling proposition; a reason why customers should select them instead of a competitor. Positioning a business can be complicated, and it can take a long time to accomplish; even decades. Nonetheless, positioning is the most productive endeavor a business owner can undertake. Understanding how your business is better and different from the competition allows you to frame the argument as to why your business should be preferred over others.

Convenience, pricing, special services, serving all faiths, or serving just one ethnic group, reception rooms, and horse drawn hearses are all factors funeral homes use to promote their competitive edge. After identifying their advantages (their unique selling proposition), execution becomes a relatively simple matter of running a few advertisements that effectively explains the competitive advantage to the public, and how that advantage better serves the consumer. The tough part is maintaining discipline; sticking with a message long enough for the advertisements to work; this is where most small businesses fail.

A good example is the better cremation societies nationally. The typical, successful minimal service cremation companies have been in business many years, communicating the same message, never straying from their core business. Many, many companies have attempted to enter this business only to fail because they did not maintain disciplined advertising and execution. Some try to expand their services to raise their average sale, while others stopped advertising long before the community learned their message.

Maintaining Discipline in the Arrangement Room

Funeral service is the only business where managers and owners, do not have (or take) the opportunity to observe associates in the execution of their job. Arrangers enter a room with families, close the door and everyone assumes they perform in a manner consistent with the firm's objectives and best interests.

Cemeteries have this same challenge with pre-need salespeople; but over 50 years they have created a means of monitoring the salesperson's behavior without observing them. Most cemeteries have a sales presentation they have refined over an extended period of time. They know when their salespeople waver from the script because their close rate will increase or decline compared to the other salespeople using the same presentation tool, and the same script. Having an established presentation system is the key to consistent performance.

Certainly, making pre-need cemetery arrangements differs from at-need funeral arrangements; but when it comes to making cremation arrangements, funeral directors working in the same building will often have radically disparate sales averages. Why? Because management has not enforced a disciplined approach for making cremation arrangements, each arranger enters the room with a family with their own agenda. Maybe they attempt to effectively communicate with the family, maybe they simply write off the family because they choose not to have a traditional funeral followed by burial.

Some licensed arrangers will argue that they should not be restrained from serving the family as they see best; and this luxury was affordable when the cremation rate was 5% or 10%; but when the cremation rate approaches 20%, 30% and even 50%, funeral businesses can not afford to have arrangers operating as the "Lone Arranger" with their own priorities and systems. At some point, management must exert itself and establish expectations. However, expectations are illegitimate without systems. Management must provide the tools necessary to accomplish specific objectives.

Funeral arrangement, particularly cremation arrangement, demands disciplined use of presentation tools to help the consumer understand the term, "personalization." Telling a family that we are going to provide a "personalized" funeral makes absolutely no sense to the average family. They expect a personalized funeral; that's why they collectively decided to set aside significant funds for a funeral or memorial. Imagine a waitress in a diner telling you she was going to serve you a "personalized lunch." You expected a personalized lunch when you decided to go out to eat; this expectation was reinforced when she gave you a menu. Why would a family anticipating a funeral bill from $4000 to $10,000 anticipate anything less than they would from the neighborhood diner?

Packaging services and creating presentation tools to facilitate communication of these packages is a means of maintaining discipline. Similarly, a plaque located in arrangement rooms stating payment terms assists arrangers in maintaining discipline relative to payment policies. Most families walk into a funeral home with no idea what funeral home payment terms are. Not having a policy or not communicating that policy is a failure of management to provide arrangers the tools they need to maintain discipline.

Maintaining Discipline in Acquisitions

Acquisition of funeral homes is probably the most common and expensive example of failure to maintain discipline. Funeral service is entering another round of consolidation, and many family-operated businesses will have multiple opportunities to acquire a competitor or funeral businesses in neighboring communities. Simply put, the margins in funeral service have declined so much, many marginal firms will attempt to sell their business. Some will represent good opportunities; others will represent traps that can burden a family business for generations. Making good acquisition decisions are a matter of discipline.

Too often individuals jump at an acquisition opportunity with too much enthusiasm. They convince themselves that they can restore the firm to its previous volume within a matter of months. Turning around a mismanaged firm takes years to accomplish; there is no short cut, and it often begins with a major remodeling costing hundreds of thousands of dollars just to get started. This is particularly true when dealing with the national corporations. The prospective buyers of these firms often have an exaggerated perspective of the value of these facilities because they have an exaggerated perception of the value of their own firm. They somehow convince themselves that they are getting a "good deal." Be realistic; the corporate deal makers have bought and sold thousands of funeral businesses; they know what a funeral business is worth. It is very unlikely a family business owner will get the better of a skilled, professional negotiator with years of practical experience.

Maintain discipline; establish your strategic priorities in advance so that you'll have criteria upon which to base your acquisition decisions. Don't jump too quickly; there are fewer sincere buyers than you might imagine. Remember, the success of an acquisition is determined before the deal is made; not afterward. If you don't know how you will make a new facility successful before you own it, the chances of it becoming a success afterward are greatly diminished.

Summary: Every licensed funeral director learned to maintain a disciplined approach when embalming when they were in mortuary school. A skilled embalmer doesn't change procedures with every case; instead they approach each case systematically. Equipment and tools are stored in an organized manner, sterilized after each use. Transferring this same discipline to matters of management would make for more productive marketing, and more profitable funeral businesses.

NOTES

NOTES

NOTES . . . .

NOTES

NOTES